THE IMAGE OF GOD

The
IMAGE
of
GOD

A THEOLOGY FOR PASTORAL
CARE AND COUNSELING

Leroy T. Howe

ABINGDON PRESS / Nashville

THE IMAGE OF GOD

Copyright © 1995 by Abingdon Press

This book is printed on recycled, acid-free paper.

Library of Congress Cataloging-in-Publication Data

Howe, Leroy T., 1936–
    The image of God : a theology for pastoral care and counseling / Leroy T. Howe.
        p.   cm.
    Includes bibliographical references.
    ISBN 0-687-00961-8 (paper: acid-free paper)
    1. Pastoral counseling.   2. Image of God.   3. Man (Christian theology)   4. Psychoanalysis and religion.   5. Pastoral theology.
    I. Title.
BV4012.2.H598   1995
253.5'01—dc20   95-35395
                                                                              CIP

95 96 97 98 99 00 01 02 03 04—10 9 8 7 6 5 4 3 2 1

MANUFACTURED IN THE UNITED STATES OF AMERICA

To Nan,

whose countenance bears God's love
delightedly and gracefully

ACKNOWLEDGMENTS

T he opportunity to serve for over ten years as pastoral counselor to the First United Methodist Church of Richardson,
Texas, afforded me many occasions for discovering the
difference that theological reflection can make in working with
distressed persons under the auspices of a lively and caring community of faith. Weekly case conferences that involved a number
of the church's ministerial staff, and attended also by persons
trained in social work, counseling psychology, and clinical psychology, helped all of us to learn from one another the complexities
and the joys of making our professional practice one way to live out
our faith in the world. The church's ministry of pastoral care also
was greatly enhanced by a network of mental health professionals
in the community, including psychiatrists at three hospitals. Members of the network showed their willingness to assist us at any time,
and often worked with our parishioners and other members of the
community whom we referred from time to time. This cooperative
effort included our pastoral care as an essential part of their
treatment. I am especially grateful to Dr. John Ogden, senior pastor
during those years, for his invitation to serve the congregation and
community. And for the support and love of the many ministers,
staff members, and laypersons who encouraged my ministry in the
congregation, I am appreciative in more ways than I can express.

Some of the case material used in this book has been drawn from
the files of the caregivers at the church, including my own. Other

materials have been contributed by several of the Doctor of Ministry students with whom I have had the privilege of working for the past twenty years. In my reconstruction of the data, in the interest of de-identification I have blended elements of several cases into each presentation. Therefore, though the dynamics of the original counseling situations are relayed faithfully, both the persons described in the narratives as well as their counselors are profiled with a literary license designed to ensure anonymity. I hope that this procedure will not make hopelessly abstract my thanks to those who have shared with me over the years a common commitment to pastoral counseling which is informed by faith and theology.

I am also indebted to the administrators of the Scholarly Outreach Award program of the Perkins School of Theology, Southern Methodist University, who made available to me a grant that helped me to begin writing this book.

CONTENTS

INTRODUCTION 11

PART I

THE IMAGE OF GOD IN THE JUDAEO-CHRISTIAN TRADITION

1. On the meaning of "origin" and "original"   24
2. Human beings "in the image of God"   27
3. "Male and female God created them": to be is to be
   in relationship   37
4. Counterpoint: The Yahwist tradition   46
5. *Imago Dei* in the Christian tradition   51
6. *Created* Nature   64

PART II

THE GOD WE WANT AND THE GOD WHO IS

1. Faith, psychology, and the wellsprings of love   80
2. God's face and God's love   85
3. Object relations theory and the idea of God   91
4. God in our image?   106

PART III

THEOLOGY IN PASTORAL COUNSELING:
THE DIFFERENCE IT MAKES

1. Some differences theology *has* made   121
2. In crises without end, amen   125
3. Sustaining the grieving   144
4. The healing of shame   155
   a. "Who told thee that thou wast naked?"   157
   b. For this, and every day, is the day of wrath   160
   c. "I blush to lift my face to you"   169
   d. "God saw all that he had made, and it was very good"   171

Notes 177

Bibliography 183

INTRODUCTION

A long with a repertoire of diagnostic resources and intervention strategies, and a level of self-knowledge complemented
by personal therapy and supervision, all competent therapists share a commitment to formulate a coherent theoretical
perspective that will give direction to their work. By means of such
a perspective, the therapist achieves more focused attention on
clients' material and is less overwhelmed by otherwise unmanage-
able data. Appeal to the chosen theoretical perspective also provides a basis for assessing the efficacy of specific therapeutic
interventions.

Pastoral counselors, too, exhibit commitment to theory which
traverses the spectrum of theoretical alternatives and fosters eclecticism in reflection on practice. From one vantage point, such
eclecticism is healthy; it can prevent theories from eroding into
ideologies that collapse the complexity of human beings and the
human environing world into a priori categorizing. However, the
frequent result of such an approach is the reduction of the pastoral
counselor's orienting perspective to a plethora of psychological
frames of reference which do not include theological resources in
their understanding of clients and their distresses.

The point of view of this book is that pastoral counseling at its
best proceeds from an informed faith sustained by involvement in
a community whose ministry to its members and in the world flows
naturally from continuous theological reflection. Of greatest im-

portance to the differentiation of pastoral counseling from other forms of psychotherapy is a Christian understanding of human existence under God, generally referred to as "theological anthropology," which is capable of informing every phase of the pastoral counselor's work. Such an understanding, formed in reference to the Christian tradition's rich insights into what it means truly to be human in a God-given world suffused with grace, is capable of providing to pastors and pastoral counselors what metapsychology makes available to psychotherapists: an operational understanding of what human beings are like; of how and why they do and do not change in reality-accommodating and reality-modifying ways; of what is realistically possible for particular human beings suffering and striving under specific conditions and in specific circumstances; and of how the attainment of realistic goals for the here and now can disclose a wider horizon of ultimate meaning and transformation, both for oneself and for the human community as a whole.

This book seeks such an understanding, formulated for the specific purpose of guiding pastors' and pastoral counselors' healing, sustaining, guiding, and reconciling ministry to persons in distress. The framework for the discussion to follow is "classical" Christian theological anthropology, which has expressed the origin, nature, and meaning of human existence in the world by some combination of propositions like the following: (1) Human beings are created in the image of God; (2) our present condition is one of having fallen into sin; and (3) in and from our fallen condition we are being both restored to our original nature and transformed to a nature more encompassing than its original character. Properly construed, propositions such as these yield an illuminating perspective on the human condition of comparable fecundity to present-day psychiatric and psychological theories.

Lost in a maze of conflicting psychological hypotheses about human existence in the world, many pastors and pastoral counselors find it difficult to articulate what is distinctive about their counseling and what difference pastoral counseling as a discipline can make to the practice of psychotherapy. In spite of its protestations to the contrary, particularly in its alleged preoccupation with "theological integration," the pastoral counseling movement in this country remains in a kind of Babylonian captivity to the latest trends in secular psychotherapies. Its training programs, its practitioners, and its practices deserve high praise for fostering competent clinical practice. But, and this is the cause for lament, it is primarily to clinical standards by which pastoral counseling competence has been measured. In earlier decades, pastoral counseling imitated the methods of Rogerian "client-centered" psychotherapy. Subsequently, transactional and gestalt therapies became the idols of the profession, followed by systems, redecision, and object relations therapies, with truncated versions of Jungianism hovering in the background. It is indeed ironic that *theological* criteria have played such a small role in assessing precisely that form of caregiving that claims to be pastoral in its very essence. For those who may be feeling some reluctance to concede this point, a few questions may be worth pondering.

Why, for instance, do pastoral counselors not as a matter of course *seek to build new relations between persons in need and a larger faith community?* Certainly, pastoral counselors must commit themselves to accept all counselees as persons of intrinsic worth and dignity. They cannot require as a condition for a counseling relationship that a counselee affiliate with any such community. Nevertheless, is it not appropriate that counselors who are intentional about providing distinctively pastoral counseling at least explore the possibility with their counselees of religious affiliation? It would not be unseemly even to recommend regular attendance at services of worship.

Counselors who do offer encouragement of this kind are often regaled with horror stories of bad experiences with organized religion. Some of these stories will provide support for the increasingly popular charge that, among the many sources of abuse which seemingly put everyone in our society at risk these days, religion may be a peculiarly venal threat to human well-being. However tempting it may be to counselors to inject early into the dialogue their own outrage over religious malfeasance and maleficence, their indignation is likely to undermine counselees' further reflection on their experiences, from which they could achieve greater openness to participating in a healthy faith community again or for the first time. Sin-ridden though every community of faith is, most contribute powerfully and posi-

13

tively to personal and spiritual growth, in ways which secular psychotherapies cannot hope to emulate.

Along with not encouraging their counselees' participation in faith communities, why do pastoral counselors also not *invite those who have come for help to explore their own faith resources and the potentially transforming power of a disciplined life of faith?* Why does pastoral counseling so frequently become mired in "contract"-oriented therapy limited from the outset to the narrow confines of the so-called presenting problem? Whether "faith resources" are conceived of in broad terms, for instance as a philosophy of life, or in more focused terms, as commitment that links people with a specific tradition of believing and acting, no one is without at least some faith resource to bring to bear upon life's distresses and calamities. Is it not one of the pastoral counselor's most important tasks to help people strengthen their faith, however confused and inadequate their faith may be at the moment? Indeed, many seek out pastors and pastoral counselors in the first place because they apprehend, however dimly, that someone whose calling is that of a curate of the soul may be better equipped to help them bring to their life-situations the richness of faith and a faith tradition.

With some counselees, pastoral counselors will find themselves beginning virtually at the beginning, struggling to guide them toward their first truly workable philosophy of life. With professed believers, the task may be nothing short of apologetics in the counseling office. A faith once held firmly may be eroding, for reasons which may or may not be adequate. Or some new spiritual awakening such as, for instance, a "life after death" experience, may challenge beliefs which proved sustaining in the past. Coming down from the mountain of a transfiguration may leave someone with such a sense of loss that reentry into the "real world" may be inordinately difficult at the moment. In such situations, what is called for is wide-ranging theological reflection, perhaps even debate. In all cases, however, the pastoral counselor should be prepared to invite those with whom she or he works to acquaint or re-acquaint themselves with at least some of the traditional ways by which the religious life is nurtured, e.g., scripture reading, worship, prayer, meditation, and service to others. Not to facilitate the exploration of these areas is to annul the most important resources any pastor or pastoral counselor has available, what in some traditions is called the "ordinary means of grace."

A third question: Why, in the inevitable and mandatory management of transference and countertransference do pastoral counselors so rarely *reflect on the transference which arises from people's hopes and expectations, mostly unconscious, for a therapeutic relationship established under "divine" auspices?* For better and for worse, the pastoral counselor-minister is a representative both of a tradition of faith and of the transcendent realities to which all traditions of faith bear their unique witnesses. It is the unconscious hope for joining with such transcendent realities that brings many to pastoral rather than to secular counselors; how counselors deal with this aspect of what is finally a pastoral relationship (namely, between a "shepherd" and those who have allowed themselves, for a time at least, to be "shepherded") will determine to a large extent the outcome of any therapy attempted in that relationship.

As many charlatan ministers have done, some pastoral counselors may exploit the unconscious yearnings in others and create a dependency that mediates neither spiritual nor psychic healing. Or, at the other extreme, pastoral counselors may avoid working with people at this level at all, either from unresolved identity questions of their own, from an excess of humility, from theological uncertainty, from fear, or from all of the above and more. Managing the transference is a task that every therapist must face, whatever that therapist's theoretical and practical orientation; transference and countertransference are ubiquitous in all relationships, and become especially intense as relationships become closer. However, the pastoral counselor's work has a unique dimension to it, precisely because of the "shamanic" character of the projections with which she or he must deal. If pastoral counselors are functioning in a genuinely *pastoral* way to their counselees, then they will be experienced, also, as priestly intercessors between counselee and God and between God and counselee. The pastoral counselor's meaning to others, and perhaps to herself or himself as well, is determined from the outset in ways that can both help and hinder the counseling.

To these three questions together, a fourth is related integrally, and has to do with the complexity of the resistance with which every pastor and pastoral counselor has to deal. As pastors and pastoral counselors seek faithfully to represent not only a tradition of belief, but ultimate reality itself, and as they offer explicit encouragement to persons to explore the resources of faith traditions and traditional means of self-discipline in faith, they will encounter a kind of resistance to their efforts that requires attention in its own right. *Remaining open to the inevitability and the necessity of such resistance,* as well as being committed to overcoming it, requires not only therapeutic skill but experience and considerable insight into oneself both as person and as professional. In the area of dealing with resistance, as with the management of transference, the pastoral counselor's task is not wholly distinguishable from that which every therapist must face. Whenever genuine change begins to occur in therapy, the therapist must manage the ensuing resistance. But the kind of resistance that pastors and pastoral counselors generate is of a distinctly different variety from what is common to psychotherapy. In pastoral counseling, resistance includes resistance to the Ultimate, even when counselees know at a deep level that only in a relationship with the Ultimate is there to be authenticity and wholeness. Why is attention to this dimension of the transference relationship so rarely discussed by pastoral counselors and in the literature of the field?

A major purpose of this book is to offer an approach to pastoral counseling that will make the discipline immediately more amenable to concerns of the sort just enumerated. The first part of the project will interpret in its import for pastoral counseling the fundamental conviction of both Judaism and Christianity that every human being is created in the image of God *by* God who has created and is creating everything in the heavens and on earth. Expressed in some such manner, this doctrine conveys what the Judaeo-Christian tradition has said most succinctly about the "essence" of humanity, and, to borrow a symbol from John Calvin used originally for another purpose, it is the lens through which pastors and pastoral counselors see human beings, in whatever condition they may present themselves, in their essential worthiness. For Christians, the guarantor of the lens's faithfulness to what is seen by means of it is Jesus Christ, whose redemptive work overcomes sin's destructive impact on the divine image in us. That "Christ's redeeming work is done" means that we may return to our own point of origin, God's creative intentions, to discover as if for the first time, who we really are: creatures of the Maker of all things, visible and invisible, who share our Creator's image and a common destiny. That indestructible image makes possible an indissoluble fellowship with God and with all of creation as grace triumphs over judgment, reconciliation over condemnation, and life over death. The ultimate goal of all pastoral counseling is to help distressed persons discover anew and cherish this divine image within themselves and others, and by so doing, to experience life in all its fullness.

This book's argument is in three parts. Part One consists of a presentation of the doctrine of the image of God in human beings that will take into account exegetical difficulties and possibilities in the relevant canonical texts, the peculiar rendering by Irenaeus of the Priestly tradition's distinctions between image and likeness, and the impact the Irenaean interpretation has had and can have on Christian theological anthropology. Part Two deals with the most important apologetic issue accompanying any exposition of the doctrine of creation in the image of God: the reasons for believing that we are created in God's image and do not, by contrast, create God in our own. Freud's influential modern articulation of an ancient view that God is a contrivance of human imagination will confront us with special cogency once the Irenaean perspective is commended for our assent. Therefore, I will offer a close examination of Freud's view, with the help of several recent object relations theorists who have reconsidered it on psychoanalytic grounds. Part Three is concerned with showing the difference a well-formed theological anthropology can make in counseling situations. Cases like these interspersed through earlier expositions for illustrative purposes will be presented and analyzed here in greater detail, with one eye on psychiatric categories for diagnosis and treatment, and the other on the kind of pastoral discernment and care that faith and theology make possible. In all of Part Three's case discussions, my aim is to bring out

17

the therapeutic power of a theological orientation in the practice of pastoral counseling.

Some further comments are necessary regarding the form in which I have presented and will present basic Christian beliefs. Prior to the seventeenth century, there was little dispute over how to interpret these affirmations. Most in the Christian community regarded doctrinal utterances as assertions about actual states of affairs, whose scope encompassed God and the whole of the created order. The community's assessment, as would be the case with respect to any propositional truth of factual import, would require clarifying their meaning vis-à-vis other propositions about the same subject matter, and putting forth the grounds, both "natural" and "revealed," for supposing any to be adequate to the way things are.

Another view of how we are to construe the beliefs of faith traditions emerged in the Enlightenment and has been especially captivating to philosophers and theologians for whom the credibility of traditional religious beliefs has come to be at issue. Whether this point of view carries the label of modernist, liberal, neo-orthodox, existential, or whatever, and however diverse its many exponents are in their own respective work, the orientation has a consistency which transcends its various permutations. It focuses on religious beliefs not so much as accounts of transcendent realities, but as expressions of inner experience, both individual and communal, of what is presumed to be the Divine. Expressive rather than descriptive in their meaning, the position states, religious beliefs require as one condition of their being understood an uncovering of the underlying experience(s) to which they bear witness. The truth of a religious belief is no longer its correspondence with objective states of affairs, but rather the faithfulness with which it renders the experience which gives rise to it.

A recent and interesting reformulation of this perspective which is attracting the attention of "post-Enlightenment" culture advocates reflects the impact of linguistic philosophy, particularly Wittgenstein's, on theology. According to this perspective, religious beliefs are neither first-order propositions nor expressions of experience, but rather are statements about how we are to *speak* of God. They are something on the order of meta-linguistic utterances whose purpose is to shape the language and the form of life of particular faith communities. Religious beliefs comprise a "grammar" of faithful speech and life and require for their understanding a level of participation in a community of faith for whom the grammar has formative as well as normative significance.

To illustrate the distinctiveness of these perspectives, I cite from I Corinthians Paul's declaration of the centrality of proclaiming Jesus' resurrection from the dead (15:12-19). For Paul and for most Christians, statements about the resurrection have to do with something that happened or did not happen to Jesus of Nazareth. Enlightenment-influenced theologies, however, tend to treat such language as about the revivification of a flagging faith in Jesus' followers. "Grammar of faith" theologies deal with the doctrine of the resurrection in terms of its function in a community of faith, e.g., to shape eschatological consciousness in the direction of remembering Jesus and anticipating feasting with him at a heavenly banquet. Which of these perspectives is the true or the more adequate one is properly a question for philosophical and systematic theologians to answer. That there *are* these diverse accounts of religious beliefs which are currently operative, however, is a datum which pastoral theology must take seriously.

Competent theologians can generate several models for understanding the basic doctrines of our own faith community because members of this community themselves presume different things about how doctrines are to function in their midst and how sound and unsound doctrine is to be differentiated. For the sake of economy of exposition, throughout this book I have chosen the more traditional way of referring to Christian beliefs about the image and likeness of God. However, as subsequent discussions of case material should make plain, it is important for pastors and pastoral counselors to be able to recognize and work with the manifestations of each perspective as they occur in counselees' faith struggles.

Though I have written this book primarily for pastoral counselors and pastors who include among their many responsibilities a focus on pastoral care, I have attempted the kind of integration of theological and psychological reflection that I hope will prove useful to "secular" psychotherapists, of whatever school, who have an interest in helping their clients deal with religious and spiritual matters. The Fourth Edition of the *Diagnostic and Statistical Manual of Mental Disorders,* published by the American Psychiatric Association in May 1994, reflects an astonishing change of orientation in the psychiatric community toward the distresses people talk about in explicitly religious terms. For generations, psychiatry has tended to regard religious faith as evidence of neurotic entanglements that patients are better off without. Practitioners who operated from such a perspective were sustained by the fond hope that as their patients became healthier by means of interventions that rarely touched upon religious material, religion itself would gradually be extinguished because these patients would go on to more productive interests and activities. Now, the same profession which has raised up this breed of religious indifferentists and antagonists, all of a sudden and before the very eyes of the secularized faithful, has done an about-face to aver that "Religious or Spiritual Problem" is an appropriate classification of a "concern" which is not a mental disorder but which, like "Marital Problem" or "Educational Problem," can be an authentic life-issue for which people may seek help from a mental health professional. This is quite remarkable. Psychologists, licensed professional counselors, marriage and family therapists, and social workers all will benefit from psychiatry's benevolent legitimizing of therapeutic work which many in these fields otherwise might cast aside, even though faith communities for millennia have provided human beings a nurturing environment in which to deal with religious and spiritual problems.

What faith communities must concern themselves with, since they generate a large number of referrals to psychotherapists and to psychiatric hospitals, is whether the new openness to religious and spiritual problems among mental health professionals will be accompanied by adequate professional preparation among those for whom working in this area will present new challenges. Of particular importance will be whether mental health professionals will have adequate opportunity to reflect on their own spiritual journeys or the absence of such journeys. Will they, as women and men of belief and unbelief, of certitude and doubt, be willing with their clients to enter into an inquiry which could be of life-changing significance to themselves as well?

PART I
THE IMAGE OF GOD IN THE JUDAEO-CHRISTIAN TRADITION

*It was you who created my inmost self,
and put me together in my mother's womb;
for all these mysteries I thank you:
for the wonder of myself, for the wonder of your
works.*
Psalm 139:13-14 (JB)

In the following sections, I present an understanding of human existence that is both faithful to the Christian tradition and directly relevant to the ministry of pastoral care and counseling. Throughout, I offer comments about the context in which I believe God now calls us to live. It is with this context in mind that I have gathered what I understand our traditions to be saying about being human in a world of which we are not the sole creators. What I hope to accomplish is to render that understanding as the truth about us in our present situation, whose discovery and appropriation represent what every pastor and pastoral counselor can affirm heartily as the ideal outcome of all soul-care. Central to a Christian understanding of human existence is the conviction that God is at work re-creating the whole of humanity as a single family whose members share a common calling to care for the created order. But our sense of partnership wanes with the failure to restrain our impulses to dominate, and solidarity with all human beings is everywhere eclipsed by oppression and enslavement. Nevertheless, we continue to yearn for a truly caring society as the harvest of a genuinely meaningful historical process. I believe this yearning to be especially deep today, and it is particularly important to the understanding of human existence in the world that I offer in the following pages.

(1) ON THE MEANING OF "ORIGIN" AND "ORIGINAL"

The affirmation that every human being is created in the image of God, the maker of the heavens and the earth, of all things visible and invisible, expresses the Christian tradition's understanding of what we as human beings most truly are, all appearances to the contrary notwithstanding. Our original, created nature is what we were meant to be by our Creator, whatever may be the condition in which we now find ourselves. The scriptural canon of both Judaism and Christianity frames this understanding in the language of "once upon a time," telling the story about the creation of human beings in two different ways to elicit a sense of what we are intended to be and an understanding that in the here and now, there is something not as it should be about us. The earlier account, from the "Yahwist," or "J," may date from as early as the tenth century B.C.E. For the purposes of the present discussion, the most important Yahwist material is in Genesis 2:4*b*-7. Another approach to telling about our origins, found in Genesis 1:1—2:4*a,* is five centuries later, from a "Priestly" narrative written after the Babylonian Exile. As we will see, these two accounts complement one another in ways important to theological anthropology.

The stories of our creation make plain to us that our actual condition is not our true condition; what we are like now is not what God wants us to be like. Once, as the Yahwist tells the story, human beings had opened to them the possibility of completely embodying God's own perfection in the ways appropriate to their finitude. However, instead of accepting with gratitude and obedience this possibility, and the life in Paradise its realization would ensure, they willfully chose a life of their own devising, miring themselves and all future generations in a world fraught with pain, suffering, danger, and death.

Though the canon of scripture has encouraged every generation of faithful Jews and Christians to dwell seriously upon the difference between what we as human beings are and what we can and are meant to be, it has proved distracting to interpret the disjunction between our created and actual nature in terms of a falling away from a prior condition. When used uncritically, the biblical stories depict our created human nature as a state of perfection lost in prehistory, from which all creatures have fallen and to which they somehow must return. All available evidence suggests, however, that the earliest stages of creaturely existence were anything but what we have imagined them to be. What lies just beyond the mists of prehistory is a threatening, insecure world whose constitutive principle is survival and conflict the unrelieved consequence. And this is the kind of world that has been present from the first appearance of distinctively human beings on the planet.

How shall we reconcile Genesis with this picture? Modern theology attempts a reconciliation by positing that the "image of God" believed to be in human beings at their creation refers to a set of possibilities that God has been seeking to actualize throughout all of history. From this standpoint, the human condition is not a "having-fallen-away-from," but rather an "on-the-wayness." Human beings are not *yet* perfected; men and women still struggle to participate in God's perfecting of them and of the created order in which they live, and the struggle often takes the form of resistance and refusal. Human perfection remains to be achieved in the future; it does not represent a lost heritage from the primordial past. Fetching as this proposal might seem in an era enamored with progress of any kind, the theological problem it presents, however, is formidable. The Genesis stories do not offer the slightest hint that the beginning is *only* the beginning of a narrative whose subsequent chapters will wholly overshadow the way things were.

A simpler way of dealing with this issue is to reflect upon another meaning for "original" which does not depend on ideas about an earliest time. What makes such reflection possible is precisely the power of the metaphor of "fall" itself to render captivatingly that we *are,* here and now, at odds with ourselves. In the language of faith: those who truly understand the human condition live with the sometimes inconsolable remorse that we persistently fail to achieve what our Creator aspires for us. We are in the here and now "falling" short of what we are meant to be by our Creator, and as a result, we are perpetually in conflict with ourselves and our neighbors as well as with God. In the language of modern-day psychotherapy: behind the pallid language of "disorder" that is currently the rage in psychiatric circles, abides the ancient term *neurosis,* dividedness, as in a household divided against itself. Our present condition is, in the whole, neurotic. One sign of how deep the neurosis goes is the intensity of the efforts many now put forth to avoid the pain of understanding that our lives are meant to be lived differently than we are now living them.

What, then, can an "original," created nature mean if not what we were once upon a time? The answer lies in the more encompassing understanding of our "original" nature as what we are "principally," bound by and to principles intended to structure our present ways of living. To express the point by means of a correlative term, what we were "originally" is what we *are,* "archaically." As does *principium, arche* points not merely to something that is first in a series, or to antecedent conditions believed to be somehow determinative of present behavior through a chain of causal sequences, but also and more important to a normative standard by which we are constituted and for which we exist at all.[1] What is truly archaic in us always, and not only at the beginning, influences and even shapes our feelings, thoughts, decisions, and actions. Conscious attention to our archaic nature creates the possibility of an intentional alliance between what we choose to be and do and what we otherwise would be formed to be and do. Failure to so attend makes it impossible to integrate our archaic nature with our daily living and forces the archaic into taking on a life of its own within and between us.

Many modern accounts of the human psyche speak eloquently of the archaic elements in us. Most, however, fail to probe the archaic at its deepest levels. For example, some remain content to construe the archaic psyche as the residue of unresolved conflicts in the family of origin, and promise us wholeness only once these conflicts are brought to conscious attention and worked through. The moral earnestness of the working-through process in psychoanalytically influenced psychotherapies bears more than passing resemblance to the pathos attending the pursuit of righteousness in God's sight through obedience to the Law. Other approaches purporting to dig deeper into the human psyche claim to have unearthed below the surface of personal and interpersonal life a repository of arche-*types,* constellations of psychic energy and symbols of human possibilities. These archetypes press for integration with conscious processes while they also lure us toward the finally unfathomable transpersonal depths that they can only imperfectly represent. What the working-through of previously unresolved and presently repressed intrapsychic and interpersonal conflicts is to psychoanalytically oriented approaches to the archaic, the integration of archetypal material in the service of individuation is to Jungian-based theories.

In both of these views, the archaic in us is both an impediment to and the wellspring for *self*-creation. Neither view, however, contributes positively toward our seeing ourselves as creat*ed* beings, by One who intentionally and lovingly dwells within, among, and around us as the source, center, and end of our existence that, paradoxically, remains distinctively our own, even as it bears a summons to live in community with all of God's creatures. As Jung came to believe that Freud had not reached the depths of the archaic by means of his method of psychoanalysis, the Christian tradition must draw a similar conclusion about the Jungian interpretation of the archaic. According to the Christian perspective, from the beginning and forevermore human beings differ from all other creatures in our likeness to the Creator of everything, on the basis of the divine image we bear. It is this image that is truly archaic, truly formative of our being. A well-formed understanding of this aspect of the doctrine of creation is foundational to any theological orientation to which correlative psychological orientations are to be subsumed, at least if pastoral counseling is to be distinctively pastoral in its approach. The image of God in human beings is the culmination of the created order that was, is, and always will be pronounced good by its Creator. We are now origin-ating in that image.

(2) HUMAN BEINGS "IN THE IMAGE OF GOD"

In both Jewish and Christian theology, the starting point for understanding what it is to be human is the affirmation that human beings are created in the image of God. This affirmation is developed always and finally in reference to the Priestly tradition in the book of Genesis, a tradition forged during the Babylonian exile. For purposes of the discussion to follow, the relevant texts are:

1:26 Then God said, "Let us make human beings in our image, after our likeness . . . "

5:1 On the day when God created human beings he made them in his own likeness.

5:3 [Adam] begot a son in his likeness and image . . .

9:6 Anyone who sheds human blood, for that human being his blood will be shed; because in the image of God has God made human beings. (REB)

The Hebrew text makes no distinction between "image" and "likeness" (*selem* and *demuth*); thus, there is no particular significance to be drawn from the omission of "image" at 5:1 or of "likeness" at 9:6. However, in the Septuagint (LXX), the Greek version of the Hebrew canon begun in Alexandria during the second century BC, the corresponding Greek terms carry different meanings, and as we will see subsequently, Christian theologians will make much of the distinction.[2] The point of the Septuagint's distinction seems to have been to bring out the differences between an exact reproduction and a less specific sort of resemblance.

The prepositions translated as "in" and "according to," in both Hebrew and Greek formulations, suggest several different facets of our relationship with God, even though as a whole their intent is simply to affirm that we resemble our Creator. The facets are worth exploring, however, first with respect to our creation *in* the divine image. A characteristic Christian use of the preposition extols our Creator as that One "in whom we live, and move, and have our being." Living "in" God, or "in" God's image, however, admits of more than one interpretation, even though the history of Old Testament interpretation rarely takes this into account. One of its frequently overlooked passages, for instance, is the elegy on the transitoriness of life in Psalm 39. The major theme of the psalm is how the wicked seem to prosper while those who strive for righteousness often are no better off for having done so. Particularly cogent for our purposes are verses 4-6:

> LORD, let me know my end, and what is the measure of my days;
> let me know how fleeting my life is! Behold, thou hast made my days

a few handbreadths, and my lifetime is nothing in thy sight. Surely every man stands as a mere breath! Surely man goes about as a shadow! Surely for nought are they in turmoil; man heaps up, and knows not who will gather! (RSV)

The word rendered at verse 6 as "shadow" is precisely the word previously encountered as "image." Alternative renderings for *selem* in Psalm 39:6 include "mere phantom," "nothing," "breath," or even "dream." A similar usage occurs at Psalm 73:19-20—"How they are destroyed in a moment, swept away utterly by terrors! They are like a dream when one awakes, on awaking you despise their phantoms." In this setting, however, it is the wicked who are mere dreams or phantoms, and as such, they only appear to succeed. In Psalm 39, *all* are like this, and so verse 13 brings that psalm to a close on a despairing note: "Look away from me, that I may know gladness, before I depart and be no more!" Later, James 4:13-15 will capture precisely this sense of who we are as human beings in the image of God:

> Come now, you who say, "Today or tomorrow we will go into such and such a town and spend a year there and trade and get gain"; whereas you do not know about tomorrow. What is your life? For you are a mist that appears for a little time and then vanishes. Instead you ought to say, "If the Lord wills, we shall live and we shall do this or that." (RSV)

Christian theology has heavily stressed the exalted status of human beings: cf. Psalm 8:5—"Yet thou hast made him little less than God, and dost crown him with glory and honor" (RSV). A major consequence of such an affirmation is that by taking it with utmost seriousness, we create for ourselves an almost insuperable difficulty comprehending the facts of sin. How could creatures bearing such an exalted status possibly sin? One way to cope with this difficulty is to complement self-congratulation with that side of ancient Hebrew thinking which speaks so eloquently about the phantasmic side of our nature. Though we are indeed like God, we also exist "in" the unfathomable obscurity of God's holiness, in the shadow-side of the One who commands light to shine in the darkness. Part of that very darkness is the shadow that the God of light casts, and precisely where God casts that shadow, there we "are." Thus, however earnestly we may feel that our proper place is in the light, close to the One who is the light of the world, by remaining aloof from the shadows we alienate ourselves from a vital part of our humanness.

The suffering, pain, evil, and even death that we encounter in the created universe have been "explained" in our tradition typically either as the appropriate consequences of human sinfulness, or as the inevitable results of existing in a finite order that imposes intractable limits on human possibilities, or as some combination of both.[3] The Psalmist suggests, instead, that there is a shadow side to our existence whose roots are in God's own shadow. Associating God's holiness with God's shadow as well as with God's transcendent goodness can help us to better understand not only the perduring distresses that accompany life in the world, but also the threatening aspects of our very closeness to God. For who has not wondered at times whether the source of her or his being is not also in some way a Destroyer? The One who nourishes us also seems bent on consuming us. The very scriptures that convey to us God's covenant with the descendents of Noah never to flood the earth again are replete with threats of a divine rage so overflowing as to consume the righteous and the unrighteous alike. Will there be mercy to those who strive for righteousness when God's fury is unleashed against all who have displeased? And yet, wholly "outside" the Source of our being, there is only non-being. Our existence (*existere*) is a standing-out-from the being of God, "in" the negativity of the divine shadow as well as in the glorious effulgence of the divine light. From this standpoint, the otherwise strange and repugnant forms of understanding (*dianoia*) that psychiatry has named *para*noia can be seen to reflect a deep awareness that insecurity and threat characterize an essential aspect of our divinely bestowed nature. Paranoid "disorders" are signs in human experience of an essential condition of shadowedness that never will submit to "cure." What Paul might have said in this regard is: if God is for us *and* against us, whom *else* need we fear?

Rachel *is a frail, gaunt, and disheveled seventy-year-old woman who traveled across town by municipal buses, transferring twice, in order to attend a seminar on dealing with loneliness led by the pastor of a mid-sized Protestant church located downtown. The hurt in her face moved the group deeply, as Rachel seemed to absorb fully the pain of others. Only the pastor noticed that Rachel shared little of herself with the group. Several days after the seminar concluded, Rachel came by the church office to leave a small donation for hunger relief. Noticing her from his office, the pastor invited Rachel to come in for a chat.*

After expressing profusely her gratitude for the pastor's leadership of the seminar, Rachel then began to pour out a story to which the pastor was uncertain how to respond. Dramatically, she told of years of strife between her daughter and son-in-law, their harassment of her, and their breaking into her apartment to take many of her prized possessions for themselves. She proclaimed it ironic that it had been close relatives who had robbed her, since she had been experiencing for some time noises at her door late at night, strange "dark" men running down her stairs and around her apartment complex, and vague noises on the roof. When the pastor asked Rachel whether she had talked with anyone about these odd happenings, she unleashed a tirade first against the apartment manager who was "in on all the goings on" and then against all the Black people in her neighborhood who were working on a plan to burn out the families who were not Black. So frightened had Rachel become that she began a practice of leaving her apartment early each morning, traveling by bus to a town sixty miles away to spend the day wandering, and then returning just before dark. She expressed fear that some of the Blacks had discovered what she was doing, were following her, and soon would attack her and leave her for dead in the other town.

Early in his conversation with Rachel, the pastor opted for a strategy of empathic listening, hoping that his caring presence would be a calming influence on a woman whose level of agitation seemed to be escalating from moment to moment. Soon, however, he found himself caught up in Rachel's story, uncertain about what to believe and not believe, anxious for Rachel's well-being, and desirous of discovering some course of action which might break the cycle of terror into which her life seemed to have fallen. Later, reflecting upon his experience, the pastor became aware of how caught up he was in Rachel's seeming helplessness and attending anxiety and of how little Rachel's rages and caricaturing of others seemed to be bothering him.

Evidently, Rachel found in the pastor the kind of sympathetic ear for which she was searching. As she arose to leave, she asked if she might come back to talk some more. The pastor responded with a warm invitation to do so, "anytime."

Several weeks later, upon returning to the church from visiting parishioners in the hospital, the pastor met Rachel in the outer office as she was sorting out some clothes to be left for the church's clothing bank. Aware of his eagerness to see Rachel, the pastor invited her to have coffee with him while they visited some more. With head bowed in a gesture of gratitude, Rachel somewhat timidly accepted.

Following the first sip of her coffee in the pastor's office, Rachel began railing against "money-hungry psychiatrists" who were "trying to put her away." Only a social worker at the local hospital really understood her, and it was she who tried to explain things to the police, who now were so much in collusion with her daughter and son-in-law that they would not answer her calls for help anymore. While running through his head the names of hospital staff he might contact for more information on Rachel, the pastor suddenly was aware that she had changed the conversation topic and now was sharing delightedly her participation in the handbell choir of a colleague's church and that she was attending Sunday services in still another Protestant church close to downtown and not easily accessible to her. The pastor realized that he knew nothing about Rachel's own religious background and was surprised to hear that she had been Jewish all her life.

In the midst of another round of character assassination, this time including Black Muslims, Roman Catholic priests, New York politicians, and police in general, Rachel quickly mentioned, as if in passing, the grief she had lived with since the time her son in New York told her she could not live with him and his family. At the end of the coversation, Rachel told the pastor of the misery of her marriage to a "good Jew" who followed the Torah to the letter but beat her regularly. The forty-four-year marriage ended with her husband's death.

As Rachel was leaving the church, the pastor became aware of how far astray his strategy of empathic listening had gone, of how overwhelmed he felt in the face of Rachel's suffering, and of how devoid he was of ideas about how to help her. He seemed fearful of moving too far into the shadows in which Rachel dwells. Indeed, Rachel's sense of shadowedness seemed well nigh impenetrable by his brand of cheerful, forward-looking pastoral care.

Being created in the image *and* shadow of God truly is a mixed blessing. The more aware we are of the shadows that envelop our own lives, the more painful it is to consider that other creatures roam more freely than we do in the light that God casts over all things. Johannine theology revels in such light, positing in God no darkness at all. But for the Psalmist, there is an exquisite attunement both to light and to the shadows that light casts. It is in these shadows that human beings also exist. The Johannine tradition's God of Light may in fact be blind to the very shadow that God's own being necessarily leaves behind. But the God of Moses seemed fully aware of what he was asking of his chosen when he demanded that they hold their gaze from him until he had passed by. For it is in the shadows, toward God's back side, that we are called to exist. Our knowledge that this is so sometimes seems more than we can bear. Will the creatures of light accommodate, or only condemn, the denizens of the shadows? Perhaps they will only pathologize shadowedness in the interest of unveiling impressive therapies posturing to help people dispel the shadows that haunt them. But there can be no help for the Rachel in all of us unless we respect both the profundity and horror of life's shadow-side, as well as the pathos that accompanies every human effort to withstand it: "Thus speaks Yahweh: A voice is heard in Ramah, lamenting and weeping bitterly: it is Rachel weeping for her children because they are no more" (Jer 31:15 JB).

As the Hebrew texts tend to refer to human beings created "in" the divine image, the Septuagint speaks of our creation "according to" (*kath*) that image. The latter preposition also is worth reflecting upon. Most basically, it conveys that we are like God through our having been fashioned to be so, that we are "after the fashion of" the divine image itself. And God's own being is the standard by which God has created and is creating human beings. Or we could say: the image of God is a representation of God's nature by which God fashions us and by which we continue to fashion ourselves. Though we are not *of* the divine "nature," we do share a common "nature" as human beings, and this nature has been given form in accordance with an image of that divine nature. We "are" that image insofar as God forms us in accordance with it and insofar as we imitate it and participate in it.

The introduction of metaphors such as "imitation" and "participation" may seem to some a reversion to Alexandrian Platonism at its most anachronistic. However, in light of contemporary predilections for "God-in-me" travesties of faith-language, the ancient terminology proves itself still to be fruitful. For the reality of our situation before God is better expressed in terms of our being in God than it is in terms of our having God or an image of God in us. Our being in God, however (and with this we move beyond the kind of Platonism which heavily influenced both Jewish and early Christian theology), is less a matter of some kind of direct participation than it is of exhibiting tendencies and inclinations to live "toward" God by means of acts of obedience and love. Upon this view, created "according to God's image" means created to live in the direction of God, with the divine image the standard or norm toward which we direct our lives and by which we judge whether we are living faithfully by them.

From the standpoint of recent object relations theory, to which we will turn in greater detail later, the divine image "in" us is an internalized representation of God and of God's will in accordance with which we are to live our lives with intentionality. It is also a representation of God's own image of us and of our place and purpose in the created order. In the Priestly tradition, however, the divine image is too often presented as lacking shadow, and, therefore, depth; it is unable to contain the ambivalence we feel as creatures living in God's shadow while we strive to live according to God's image. Substance without shadow, the image represents only partially the ambiguities with which the divine-human relationship is fraught.

There are other meanings which must be explored in the Priestly tradition's affirmation of a *resemblance* between human beings and God. The first points to a proper referent for "Adam" and the subject to be characterized by the resemblance. At Genesis 1:26 is expressed the intriguing formulation "let us make Adam . . . ";

here, the resemblance posited is between humanity as a whole and a heavenly court within which God is, and is concealed. With the merging of the Yahwist and Priestly accounts of creation, it became an easy matter to construe "Adam" as a proper name and to reconceptualize the divine-human resemblance as between a single man and God. Once this latter usage was taken up, however, the affirmation that the whole of humanity also resembles God could only be made by delineating the generations of the first man. The divine image now has to be communicated to future generations by virtue of an inheritance through Seth, through a process obscured in contradictory theories about how original sin and its consequences are transmitted from one generation to the next. As Seth became the archetype of inherited divine resemblance, Cain became the archetype of inherited corruption. Unhappily, Christendom even to the present day remembers Cain more vividly than it does Seth, and continues to draw the multitudes into the family of God by emblazoning on their collective foreheads the mark of Cain and by alleging a unique possession of the means for its removal. The dis-ease which the churches propose to cure, "original" sin, is in the strictest sense "iatrogenic," that is, induced by its healers. On behalf of the misled faithful today, pastoral counselors can make available the towels needed by the few who may be ready to wipe clean their own abused foreheads.

It is singularly unfortunate that Christian thinking about human nature became mired in the confusion of positing a "first man," because the most important scriptural texts for understanding human beings clearly speak of the divine image in us in terms of the whole of humanity in relation to God. As Jürgen Moltmann puts it: "It is not against his or her fellow human beings nor apart from them but only in human fellowship with them and for them that the individual can correspond to his or her destiny as created in the image of God" (1984, p. 25). It is especially to Genesis 1:26 that we must refer when asking the next questions important to understanding that and how we image our Creator: (a) with respect to what does the resemblance obtain between humanity and God?, and (b) why are human beings alone created "bearing" such a resemblance? Neither question admits of fruitful reflection if it must be thought through in reference only to some kind of resemblance between ourselves and a first human, "before." the Fall.

On the first question, the Priestly tradition appears far from definitive, perhaps because it seems to lack interest even in asking the question. The disinterest, if indeed it is disinterest, may be a necessary accompaniment of this tradition's exaltation of God's holy and unapproachable otherness. We are to trust that God has created us resembling our Creator, the tradition seems to be saying to us, but we are not to know fully what that resemblance can be. However, the tradition is not altogether silent about the resemblance. It suggests variously, for instance, that our resemblance to God includes physical form, wisdom, goodness, character, rationality, relationality, and freedom. Later in the exposition, I will draw upon these suggestions in opening a fuller discussion of our resemblance to God in terms of *capacities*.[4]

On the second question, which asks for the "whys" of our bearing uniquely a resemblance to God, the Priestly tradition is clearer than it is about the question with which we have just been dealing. Humanity is created according to God's image in order that human beings, and no other beings, can represent God (namely, re-present God, make-God-present-again) on earth. *Dominion* is the key: "and let them have dominion over the fish of the sea, and over the fowl of the air, and over the cattle, and over all the earth, and over every creeping thing that creepeth upon the earth" (Gen 1:26*b* KJV). Wolfhart Pannenberg points out the distinctively new understanding in the Priestly tradition of God's earthly representatives:

> In the ancient Near East the idea of likeness to God and that of divine sonship were the special privilege of the king and the mark of his position; only in the Old Testament were they extended to humankind generally. . . . By making the statement about the image of God in the human being the Priestly document is thus assigning the human being as such the role of king in the context of creation. (1985, p. 75)

By virtue either of a nature or a destiny created according to God's image, we are both authorized and empowered to "subdue the earth" as God would: respectfully and caringly. As Moltmann expresses the point: "human dominion over the earth includes a sense of community with the earth" (1984, p. 27). Dominion is linked with community and cooperation, and is part of our destiny to live in fellowship with God, with the human community as a whole, and with the natural order. What is essential in exercising dominion is the conjoining of authority, power, wisdom, and goodness. In particular, when power becomes alienated from wisdom and goodness, then dominion becomes domination and subduing becomes rape.

(3) "MALE AND FEMALE GOD CREATED THEM": TO BE IS TO BE IN RELATIONSHIP

In the Priestly tradition it is all of humanity, and not human beings as individuals, that bears the primary resemblance to God. "Adam" as referring to a first man is of decidedly secondary importance to "Adam" as referring to humankind. Walther Eichrodt once addressed this point in the context of discussing Israel and the "nations":

> In virtue of their creation by the one God the nations are members of a large family and the list of nations in Genesis 10, which stands alone in ancient oriental literature, gives to Israel itself, too, however conscious of its important place in history, its place among (humankind) in general, and does not claim for Israel a fundamentally different natural ability, a hereditary mobility which would contrast it with all the other nations. The Old Testament will not hear of originally inferior races, nor of a barrier between Hellenes and Barbarians, never quite overcome in the humanism of antiquity, or between masters and slaves. (1951, p. 35)

Of equal importance is the Priestly tradition's affirmation that relationships *constitute* human nature: being human is being with others. The creativity with which we are to exercise our dominion over the earth is shared creativity. We are to exercise dominion together. The Yahwist tradition speaks of relationality in its own typical storytelling style: "Then the LORD God said, 'It is not good for the man to be alone; I shall make a partner suited to him' "

37

(Gen 2:18 REB). Adam's "loneliness" includes both yearning and helplessness. He is helpless fully to exercise dominion over creation; he can name the beasts God brings to him, and thereby assure their fitness in the scheme of things, but Adam is not yet fit himself. He is immobilized by longing, unable to fulfill the purpose of his creation. Both the Yahwist and the Priestly traditions together support the same key ideas: all human beings, themselves created by God to order the rest of creation, are to exercise dominion, together, over the whole and not over particular territories (*contra* "territorial imperatives") by means of a partnership entailing commitment to mutual respect, fairness, and cooperation.

Societies that like our own pursue relentlessly the optimal conditions for *individual* self-fulfillment eventually find themselves bankrupt of worthy aspirations for the society as a whole and rattled by their members' paralyzing fears of failure to achieve self-sufficiency. Such fears are fully justified. Left to our own devices to find our place in the social order, with the outcome wholly dependent on our own ingenuity, we know that when we are unable to take care of ourselves and those for whom we have assumed responsibility, we will find ourselves bereft of sources of compensation and comfort and regarded by those who have outrun us in the race of life as one more of the multitude of "social problems" with which they will have to deal. These people will add to our pain their own scornful reminders of how many opportunities we have had to make something of ourselves, and from our last bludgeoning we may succumb to the grandest delusion of all, that everyone does indeed begin equally, with the same chance for success and happiness in life. Whether our individual freedoms are understood as inalienable rights or as precious gifts conferred, their cost may still be prohibitive in a society for whom tending to the well-being of all its members is relegated to the contingencies and uncertainties of "voluntary" associations. As the volunteers celebrate their altruism, the numbers of hurting, homeless, hopeless, wasted, and lonely people continue to mount. Each is quietly reduced to the status of a welfare recipient in the eyes of the financially secure. Human beings are created for community, and nothing accomplished by way of individual fulfillment and aggrandizement can fully compensate us for the misery suffered when the structures supportive of genuine community are compromised.

Vesta is a single woman in her mid-sixties who lives by herself in an apartment complex close to the church she is considering joining. After she attended a worship service there, the pastor called on her at home. She told the pastor that she was a member of a much larger church near downtown, but felt she now needed to find a smaller and more accessible congregation. The pastor invited her to worship again, and recommended a Sunday school class. Vesta began attending worship services and the class regularly.

Several weeks later, the pastor returned for a longer visit with Vesta. He learned that she grew up just a few miles from where she was now living. Life was hard in her childhood, money was scarce, and her father struggled constantly to keep the few low-paying jobs for which he was qualified. The family was active in a Lutheran church near their working-class neighborhood. She met her husband in that church, and remained a member there for most of her adult life. She and her husband bought a house nearby, and reared their family there. She took pride in their home, spending a great deal of time maintaining it, keeping up the lawn, and developing a garden large enough to supply food for her family. Eventually, the children grew up, moved out, and settled in different parts of the country. In her mid-forties, Vesta reevaluated a number of her commitments. Her family's neighborhood had become more racially diverse, unnerving a number of residents into selling their homes and moving out. Their decisions took a considerable toll on the membership of Vesta's church. With most of her friends gone, Vesta decided to visit the larger church near downtown, with the support of her husband. They both joined. Vesta became involved in the church's music program, but her husband's interest in church activities began to decline.

Shortly after her sixtieth birthday, Vesta's husband left her with neither notice nor explanation, and soon thereafter filed for divorce. Their forty-year marriage ended just as Vesta was diagnosed with multiple sclerosis. Anticipating that she would not be able much longer to take care of her house by herself, Vesta recently sold it and moved to her current apartment. She now has recurrent pain and weakness, and is preparing for the next stage of her life in a wheelchair. Vesta is having considerable difficulty with the impending loss of her many friends and activities at the church where she still has her membership. But the buildings now are very crowded, making movement difficult, and her Sunday school class has been moved to a section of the building only accessible by stairs. Tearfully, Vesta told the pastor that she had no choice but to find a church that demanded only a short commute, had parking close to the building, and would be wheelchair-accessible. She feared not finding a close-knit community of persons who would show concern as her condition progressed. She wished her children were closer by, but expressed happiness that "they have their own lives now."

Genesis 1:27*b* proposes a startling concretization of the principle of relationality: humankind's resemblance to God is most evident in the fullness of male-female relationships.[5] When the story of the creation of woman at 2:18 and following is appended, then we have before us a normative image of human relationality in terms of a partnership whose principal sign is the bonding of male and female, and, perhaps even more startling, the progeny resulting from their unions. This latter association demands an especially close scrutiny. At Genesis 1:28 the Priestly writer relays: "God blessed them and said to them, 'Be fruitful and increase, fill the earth and subdue it' " (REB). This text raises a crucial question about the male-female relationship: what is the relation of propagation (a) to the integrity of the relationship, and (b) to the exercise of dominion? It is very difficult to bring into clear light the understanding of the male-female partnership until these questions can be cleared up and removed from the forefront of theological controversy.

With regard to the first question, it is important to remind ourselves that the text will not support the position of those who have burdened couples for centuries with the erroneous notion that offspring alone legitimate a union. Clearly, in the Priestly writing, propagation is not itself part of the divine image. In spite of their own yearning and anguish to conceive, for example, offspringless couples are not somehow less than their Creator intended for them to be. Instead, propagation is presented as a response to an invitation and not a command. The resemblance between humanity and God is not principally in terms of fecundity, even though many so-called nature religions forge just such a connection. According to the Priestly tradition, God bestows fecundity on a "nature" already fashioned to be what it is intended to be.

However, fruitfulness *is* linked with fulfilling God's purpose of dominion: "fill the earth and subdue it." Since we are created according to the image of God in order that we might have dominion over all else and exercise that dominion effectively on God's behalf, there would seem to be at least an implicit relation between propagation and the exercise of dominion, enough of a relation to suggest that it really might be part of the purpose of human nature after all to be fruitful and to increase. Perhaps there *is* a basis for affirming sexual behavior only within the context of intending conception, and that apart from an intention to be fruitful, sex, even in a loving union, defiles human nature created according to God's image.

One way of avoiding this outrageous conclusion is to argue that it tears God's invitation to be fruitful out of context and renders it as a timeless moral command. The linking of procreation and dominion obtains only "in the beginning" and "for the beginning." Today, the argument proceeds, human beings are multiplying at an obscene rate that threatens the very dominion that propagation originally was intended to serve. For any conceivable future, therefore, "fruitfulness" must be encompassed by choice, leaving to nature that which properly belongs to nature, and freedom to the *human* realm. The difficulty with this resolution is that it literalizes the mythological language of scripture and loses sight of the ongoing and sustaining power of those archaic foundations always present to and in us. If the archaic does continue to originate us, the question must still remain as to whether procreativeness is an aspect of this archaic "nature."

Another approach is to look more closely at what our archaic nature, e.g., "natural" means in the context of human reproduction. For instance, if by "natural" we mean part of our potential as human beings, procreativity would have to do with the *capacity* to produce offspring. An invitation from God to be fruitful would convey God's empowerment to fulfill the invitation. There are two major problems with defining human nature in this way. In the first place, such a view could become intolerably sexist. Many people

41

still believe that children are conceived through the woman, and are prepared to dehumanize wives in childless relationships by construing their "barrenness" as an expression of divine disfavor. In the second place, we now know too much about infertility to characterize all people's humanity too closely in terms of their child-conceiving and childbearing capacities. Many couples desiring to produce offspring find themselves confronting biological inhibitors they cannot overcome, and their suffering renders wholly implausible any general claim that God equips all to fulfill the invitation to be fruitful.

A still better way of looking at ourselves is in terms of our intentionality: specifically, as the capacity to be created and to create ourselves in the light of the intentions of others and of our own intentions for them. In this way of thinking about the matter, procreativity has to do with intending good for others and for oneself, and represents the overall mindset within which we are to enter all relationships, and not just the sexual aspects of intimate relationships. There are many ways to subdue an already filled earth besides the obvious way of further populating it with offspring. What is crucial for the integrity of intimate sexual relationships today is not only the intention to beget, but also the intention that the relationship itself will be generative of a kind of love that can be shared with all of God's creatures.[6] From this standpoint, it becomes clear how "single" people also are whole and complete human beings in their own right. The capacity for genuine engagement as male and female in fulfilling God's intentions for all humankind does not entail that every man and woman must enter into an intimate and exclusive sexual union. What is intended, instead, is that all men and women actively seek each other's well-being in faithfulness to God who is the source and end of the creative process itself. For some women and men, seeking another's well-being will include contributing to each other's sexual fulfillment, with or without offspring. For all men and women, the call is to be in partnership that seeks the well-being of all God's creatures, including the earth itself.

Contrary to the hopes of most Christians everywhere, it may no longer be possible to lift up our current ideal for the intimate union between a man and a woman as the most profound symbol of the kind of community God intends for all human beings. In the first place, many people still find it impossible to dissociate the begetting of offspring from their understanding of the purpose of marriage. Second, still larger numbers of people, surfing on the waves of pansexualism that rush ceaselessly toward the shores of contemporary cultures the world over, are unable to dissociate "the joys of sex" (now the manic pursuit of simultaneous and multiple orgasms) from their understanding of the best that marriage has to offer. Among both groups of people, there is massive confusion of the purposes of marriage with marriage's contingent outcomes.

A much more important reason, however, for the somber conjecture under consideration is the virtually unanimous consensus in modern societies that the marriage relationship should be an enduring communion between two persons that will ensure the complete satisfaction of each other's every emotional need and longing. Ironically, in the very culture that gave birth to this view, the culture of medieval chivalry, there was no misunderstanding about the impossibility of realizing such a union under the conditions of earthly existence; to attempt to do so would subject the lovers to nothing less than death. Romantic ideals had their proper place in imagination rather than in physical consummation. But the modern view of marriage fatefully puts before us the ideal and, indeed, the necessity, of realizing full, perfect, and complete communion in a relationship of intense, life-long intimacy, unperturbed by the otherwise sobering aspects of living in a pressured, conflict-ridden, competitive, and often threatening social order. Most marriages simply cannot bear the burdens of such overwhelming expectations. The "slings and arrows of outrageous fortune" can become all the more baleful when love is asked to endure through them indefinitely. And the expectation that every marriage must create a perfect union fit for heaven can prove lethal to those neither "called" to nor "gifted" for such a venture.

George seemed to his harried and overworked pastor a godsend, too good to be true. Shortly after he began attending the church, George volunteered to do a variety of clean-up projects around the property, joined a spiritual formation group, and quickly made many friends who shared with the pastor how much they thought George's presence had added to the congregation. Later, the pastor began hearing accounts of several confessions George had made to the formation group and of how many in the group had become involved in his nurture. While working together painting the exterior trim on the church's educational building, the two men had several lively conversations which filled in some of the details of George's life.

George was fifty-two years of age and married to **Lisa,** *twenty-five years younger than he. The previous winter she had left him and taken their two small children to her father's home in another state, over fifteen hundred miles away. George relayed this information in the middle of speaking of himself as "nothing but bad," as someone who had no right to live. Retired from the military at age forty-five, George met Lisa in a bar, found her eager to escape a relationship with an abusive lover, and quickly proposed marriage. Never married, and with little experience relating to women, George found Lisa's attentions flattering and welcome. With the children's births, he took on odd jobs to supplement his retirement income, but felt that Lisa was never satisfied with what he provided and that she was not particularly attracted to him. George thought it curious that he was raising some of the same questions about himself in his marriage that he remembered his father sharing with him about his own marriage. He acknowledged his tendency to be very controlling of Lisa, and that he lost his temper frequently, with both Lisa and the children. He lamented Lisa's lack of interest in "spiritual things," that she would not attend church with him, and that she was opposed to his efforts to have the children baptized.*

Some weeks later, George informed the pastor that Lisa and the children had come home, and the pastor promised to drop by for a visit the next morning. At 4:00 A.M. he received a call from George's next-door neighbor that there was "a big fight going on" between George and Lisa and that "all hell was breaking loose." The neighbors were active church members and agreed to meet their pastor at the couple's house rather than to call the police. When he arrived, the pastor learned that Lisa had threatened to kill George and that other neighbors had already taken the children into their care. Someone had called the police, and they arrived as the pastor was finishing up his first work with the couple. Later, the police filed a domestic violence report.

The pastor took notice of the black and blue spots on Lisa's arms and face, and the fact that George and Lisa were communicating only by hurling accusations and insults at each other, while the children were yelling to no one in particular. The immediate issue seemed to be money. The pastor promised to arrange financial assistance through the church and to help the couple learn to communicate better with each other. George agreed to stop the physical abuse of his wife. Many in the congregation reached out to the couple in love and support. Lisa came to church services with George, and agreed to have the children baptized. Later, George spoke to the congregation during a Sunday worship service and testified to the changes God had brought about in him. Lisa appeared genuinely moved by her husband's witness, and the congregation was uplifted by what they saw happening in the couple's life together.

Three days following the service, the pastor received a call that George and Lisa were fighting again on their front lawn, screaming and throwing things at each other. By the time he arrived, both George and Lisa had drawn blood, but the pastor was able to break up the fight. He demanded that they undergo family counseling, and the couple agreed. Lisa shared that she had been abused as a child, especially by her mother, that she was beaten by every lover she had ever taken, and that she was furious with George over his temper and his failure to provide adequately for her and the children. George told the pastor for the first time about his mother's leaving his father and that he feared he would also be abandoned by any woman he let himself love deeply. In the couple's living room, the pastor offered prayer and left the calmed situation to arrange the family counseling.

When he returned to the church, the pastor's secretary greeted him with the alarming news that Lisa had locked herself in a bedroom and had mixed pills with liquor in an attempt to kill herself. George had beaten her shortly after the pastor left their home. A week after Lisa's return from psychiatric hospitalization, George left home with nothing in his possession. There were several empty prescription bottles in the bathroom sink. A police search through the nearby woods failed to find George, and he has not subsequently been found.

If present-day expectations for the institution of marriage have become formidable obstacles to that institution's symbolizing what God intends for all relationships, then what is happening today in male-female relationships as a whole raises even more questions about whether our maleness and femaleness can shed *any* light on what it can mean to be with and for others. That men and women are to live and work with and for each other seems to have become an especially pernicious idea, incendiary to the moral sensibilities of women outraged over exploitations of them the world over, and terrifying to men who have only lately embarked confusedly on a quest for clues into how they might fit into a world that they perceive bemoans their existence. Preoccupations with issues of gender identity, gender differences, and gender equity have become the most politically correct way to rationalize regression into that twilight world of social existence in which human beings are reduced to categorial entities only, belonging either to the group of those like us or to the group of those not like us, and therefore not liked *by* us. Between men and women especially, there now lies the threat of *jihad*.

Whatever may be the final outcome of the current efforts to dismantle all cultures and cultural institutions whose arrangements between men and women fail to pass decreed litmus tests, one fundamental truth about human beings remains that will have to be confronted. It is that what makes us human is not so much what is "in" us (for instance and especially, whether we are "peniled" or "vulvaed"), as what "between" us will make it possible for us, together, to fulfill a common calling and destiny. God's promise to Abraham surely includes as part of the re-creation of one human family the reconciliation of women and men everywhere.

(4) COUNTERPOINT: THE YAHWIST TRADITION

The Priestly tradition in the Old Testament has decisively shaped Christian theological thinking about human nature, so much so that no exposition from a Christian perspective of what it means to be human can hope even to approach adequacy without taking into account that tradition from the outset. But it is also important to remember that in both the Jewish and the Christian canons of scripture, there are *two* distinctive, and distinctively different, depictions of God's creation of human beings, and in them, two different pictures of the beings created. Certainly, the

Priestly account is the normative one, but the Yahwist understanding has its own insights to contribute to the canon, as both corrective and balance to what is actually the later of the two traditions in order of composition. Before we turn explicitly to the Christian appropriations of the Priestly tradition, therefore, it will be helpful to pause and look briefly, for purposes both of contrast and completeness, at the Yahwist account of human nature and God.

The relevant text is Genesis 2:7: "The LORD God formed man of dust from the ground, and breathed into his nostrils the breath of life; and man became a living being" (RSV). This is a quite different way of speaking about human nature from that of the Priestly tradition, whose theology of human existence emphasizes form, structure, permanence, closeness with God, community, and, finally, active mastering (cf. "subdue," "fill," "achieve dominion"). By contrast, the Yahwist's is a theology of dust-formed life that looks at human nature in its fragility, vaporousness, and transience. It is this tradition which is expressed at Psalm 104:29*b,* "thou takest away their breath, they die, and return to their dust" (KJV). This tradition is paralleled at Job 34:14-15, "If he were to turn his thoughts inwards and recall his life-giving spirit, all that lives would perish on the instant, and man return again to dust" (NEB).

Rather than on our closeness with God, the Yahwist focuses on our closeness to earth: from it we are fashioned and to it we will return. While the Priestly tradition associates earth's matter with the primordial chaos, and exalts God for the transformation of that chaos into an ordered world, the Yahwist celebrates the fact that human beings are formed from this very *un*transformed matter. In place of the theme of active mastering, the Yahwist inserts the theme of grateful receiving. Adam must tend what is given to him in paradise, but there is nothing he is required to subdue, and, indeed, nothing which *can* be subdued. Sometimes, it is difficult to accept gratefully some of the conditions of our material existence, most especially when they include inexplicable suffering, unanswered questions, and death well before the promised "threescore years and ten."

47

In the wisdom that guided the formation of the scriptural canon, the Priestly and the Yahwist traditions represent ways of looking at ourselves that are, together, necessary to fully do justice to all that we can identify in ourselves as our created nature. The closeness of their association in the organization of the canon suggests a certain clarity that emphasizing one perspective at the expense of the other can lead to disastrous misunderstandings of our humanness. By holding these meanings in creative tension, we have available to us the means for correcting the tendency to see ourselves only in one way.

In the so-called developed nations of the world, which are benefiting lavishly from the myriad "advances" of Western technology with its bureaucratizing of all social life, alliances with the Priestly tradition's coronation of humanity as earth's rulers will lend much needed support to the illusory values of control and mastery that drive our present-day highly competitive, acquisitive lifestyles. Incorporating only this part of our tradition carries with it the dangers of reinforcing life commitments that require for their sustenance a high degree of self-protectiveness, remoteness, suspiciousness, defensiveness, and at the outer edge of functionality, the addictive behaviors that are the insignias of all too many of the "movers and shakers" who feel that they must disguise their insecurities, anxieties, and chronic disappointments at all costs.

Our culture embodies to the fullest that kind of exaltation of humanity's closeness to and status before God that tempts people to assume a posture of domination over others and over nature and to assume that only those who can achieve a certain level of mastery and control of their lives, not to mention wealth, will be favored in the grand scheme of things. Far too much misery has been perpetrated in the name of a positive philosophy of human existence in the world not properly qualified with the help of a complementary perspective such as that in the Yahwist texts, which quite literally bring us back and down to earth, to the *humus* in association with which life-renewing humility, nurtured in good humor, may thrive.

The grandiosity that makes its appearance with such regularity among dominating classes also infects revolutionaries whose self-appointed mission is to bring about a massive shift of power in the

governance of human societies, always, of course, for the better-
ment of all. Assured of their cause's righteousness, and legitimated
in their vitriol that they pour indiscriminately upon all whom they
perceive to disagree with them for whatever reason, seekers after
their own versions of justice all too frequently parade a presump-
tuousness which, like a lava flow, presently is swallowing whole
subcultures around us and burying our collective psyche in fratri-
cidal conflicts between disparate groups of self-righteous people
each with its own peculiar sense of entitlement. The current language of social and cultural self-aggrandizement whirls around a
dialectic of oppression and liberation, with the honors going to
those who can establish themselves as the most "wretched of the
earth." Assisted by liberation theologians thriving on moral passion
and happily enslaved by the very kinds of ideological thinking they
so resent in others, oppressed people everywhere vie for what to
them is their just due, and are prepared to put to rout not only
their own enemies, but everyone they think may be oppressing
anyone else. In the solidarity with the oppressed, suffering generates its own privileged classes and becomes the royal road to divine
favor. Apparently, as human history moves out of its infancy, God
is experiencing a change of heart regarding his preferred companions on earth, now choosing to throw in with only the downtrodden
and to withdraw favor from all who have not suffered enough.

But struggling to overthrow domination by means of raw power,
seductive influence, expertise, gifts, communication of favor, or
whatever merely excites the craving in all of us to master things and
bring them under our control. The oppressed, too, distort and even
pervert our God-bestowed calling to tend the earth caringly and
respectfully. Whether in the interest of overcoming or of sustaining
oppression, the rationalization of our transgressions against other
creatures by means of indefensible claims of superiority and supremacy conferred by none other than God leads inescapably to
tyrannous relationships and to indifferentism toward anything and
anyone not fitting into our own grand designs. How unseemly to
the overly righteous on both sides is the idea so treasured by the
Yahwist that all of us must return one day, of all places, to the earth,
from which we will posture no more.

The Yahwist's account of our creatureliness is an indispensable corrective to our proclivities for seeing ourselves as gods. It can be disastrous, however, not to see this account as a corrective and, instead, to read out of it the sole and last word about what it means to be human. Then, our fragility, vaporousness, and impermanence will become all there is in and between us. For some, this will mean that everything that is exciting in and to us can vanish from our lives in an instant, that our most profound hopes are but yearnings spawned from illusion, and that our deepest commitments and loyalties will require enormous expenditures of limited, precious life energy without the satisfactions that would make the investments worthwhile. Contemplation of such prospects, without a compensating perspective, can lead to a sense of hopelessness and meaninglessness, and a corresponding withdrawal of interest in present-day living. Cynicism and despair are the most frequent outcomes:

> What does anyone profit from all his labour and toil here under the sun? Generations come and generations go, while the earth endures for ever.
> The sun rises and the sun goes down; then it speeds to its place and rises there again. The wind blows to the south, it veers to the north; round and round it goes and returns full circle. All streams run to the sea, yet the sea never overflows; back to the place from which the streams ran they return to run again. All things are wearisome. No one can describe them all, no eye can see them all . . . What has happened will happen again, and what has been done will be done again; there is nothing new under the sun. (Eccl 1:3-9 REB)

Besides despair, however, there is another and quite different kind of response possible to the contemplation of life's evanescence: the response of "eat, drink, and be merry, for tomorrow you may die." Both unawareness of and acute sensitivity to our fragility and impermanence can lead to the same kind of fascination with the earthly at the expense of appreciation for the sublime. But awareness casts a somber hue over unbridled sensuality, and attachments of the moment become "sicklied o'er" with the recognition that the only sure mode of existence for humans is precisely that of living for the moment. Living for the moment, even when the moment is received gratefully as a divine gift, can drive us to a mode of seeking in diversions a cloak for either our sloth or our despair, unless it is balanced by a sense of responsibility for participating in the ordering of all creation as a response to a divine summons, however long or short may be the time given us.

Together, then, the Priestly and the Yahwist accounts of human beings created by God offer us a wholistic understanding of what it means to be human by gathering and juxtaposing two ways of looking at human nature which, in spite of appearing to be polar opposites, perform complementary functions for our under-standing of ourselves. It is especially important that we appreciate the power of each to compensate for the incompleteness of the other. The Christian tradition, however, has concentrated almost exclusively on the Priestly texts, as we shall now explore.

(5) *IMAGO DEI* IN THE CHRISTIAN TRADITION

In the New Testament, two texts are especially illuminative of the process by which the Old Testament informed early Christian thinking about human existence before God and in the world. The first is Colossians 3:9-10: "Do not lie to one another, now that you have discarded the old human nature and the conduct that goes with it, and have put on the new nature which is constantly being renewed in the image of its Creator" (REB). This letter transforms radically the Priestly tradition. Here, the image of God has become human nature redeemed by Christ and no longer human nature in its "original" form. *Eikon* is still used in the sense of a repre-sentation of a prototype, but the prototype now is defined as Christ rather than as that nature with which human beings originally were endowed by their Creator: "*He* is the image of the invisible God; his is the primacy over all creation" (Col 1:15 REB, emphasis mine).

A second New Testament text which is instructive for our pur-poses is James 3:9. The context is a series of criticisms of improper uses of speech, and it includes a discussion of many harmful uses of the power of the tongue. "We use [the tongue] to praise our Lord and Father; then we use it to invoke curses on our fellow-men, though they are made in God's likeness" (REB). In using *homoiosis,* James alludes to the Hebrew *demuth* rather than *selem,* "likeness" rather than "image," although it is not likely that the writer saw any real difference in the words, even as the Hebrew tradition did not. What is especially interesting is the preference for the phrasing of Genesis 5:1, 3 over that of Genesis 1:26. Does this mean that James preferred to construe "Adam" as singular rather than as collective? We have no way of knowing. An additional difficulty is that the translation of the Greek text leaves us with a decision to make in the exegesis of the text's meaning. In the verse from the REB above, the thought is thoroughly congruent with traditional Hebrew thinking. So rendered, James is referring to an original, created nature. But the Greek text admits of an alternative translation, to wit: "men, who *have come to be* according to the likeness of God" (italics mine). If this is the preferred rendering, James would seem to be writing about redeemed humanity, in precisely the way that the author of the Colossians letter does.

Clearly, a distinctively Christian understanding of the image of God in human beings is beginning to emerge in the New Testament period, which, in addition to its inclusion of christological references important to subsequent theological reflection on the nature and work of Jesus as Christ, points toward a new way of distinguishing the divine "image" from the divine "likeness" in human beings. This new understanding unfolds most fully in the thought of the second-century theologian *Irenaeus, Bishop of Lyons* (c. 130–202). Though his views are solidly anchored in the Priestly tradition of the Old Testament, Irenaeus exhibits no hesitation in using this tradition's terminology in new ways, most especially by elaborating upon a distinction between "image" and "likeness" that will move the Christian tradition to an altogether new plane of understanding human nature.

In our very formation as human beings, Irenaeus wrote, we have received God's image, and in that image reside our capacities for rational thought, for making decisions freely, and for fellowship with our Creator. In addition to having been created in the image of God, we are also created "like" God. Our likeness to God, however, expresses our future development and not our present nature. We receive this divine likeness through the Holy Spirit, as the Holy Spirit works in and with us to make us perfect. We bear the divine image already, insofar as we are rational beings responsible for our decisions and capable of sustaining communion with God. But our likeness to God remains a destiny to be realized, and can be realized only as our spirit, longing, and striving for God, is received and transformed by God's own spirit. To become more and more like God and in communion with God, our Creator, is our purpose for being.[7]

Irenaeus conceives our created nature not in terms of an original perfection mysteriously lost in some kind of primordial catastrophe, but rather in terms of an infancy nurtured toward maturity by a loving Creator who has set before us the task of choosing how and whose we will be. In this context, he presents the difference between "image" and "likeness" by means of a subtle analogical argument based upon distinguishing two ways of being a son to a father. The first is the way of natural generation and birth, and the second the way of conforming one's life to that of one's natural father. Irenaeus's argument can be expressed faithfully in a more contemporary idiom. We are born to a set of parents whose biological heritage we bear simply by virtue of being their offspring. The extent to which we really "turn out" like them, however, is a function of the extent to which we set out to do so, deliberately performing just those actions that will make us more like our parents. Being a "chip off the old block," or the "spitting image" of a parent or some other family member, is primarily a volitional rather than a genetic matter. The all-important theological conclusion Irenaeus reaches with the help of his analogy is this: all human beings are children of God the Creator in the first sense, and God desires that all will be children in the second; but only some will become children in that second sense, for not all will be obedient in and affirming of the "natural" relationship. Irenaeus's position is that human beings are created in the image of God in the first sense of the analogy, and in the likeness of God in the second.

To be sure, Irenaeus's language is not as uniform as the previous paragraphs would suggest. Sometimes, he seems to be thinking of the divine image in us as simply our reason and free will, and our divine likeness as some sort of supernatural endowment. And at least at one point, he appears to lose sight of the distinction altogether, referring both to our image and our likeness being lost in Adam and restored in Christ. But as J. D. Kelly commented, surely this is an overstatement, "since the image must have persisted in some degree" (1960, p. 171). Kelly's interpretation opens out onto an immense range of theological controversy that will be identified presently. Before dealing with that controversy specifically, though, I will add the clarification of image and likeness offered by Maurice Wiles:

> The Word, who in the incarnation became what we are in order to make us what he is, is the same Word which was operative in the original creation, the one in whose image the first man was made. Adam was created an innocent child, intended to grow up into the full image and likeness of God. That development was arrested by man's sin and by the death that follows from it. But at the incarnation the development is set in motion once again; a new and firmer link is established between man and the divine life; the Word continues his creative work in a way which will no longer be thwarted. Irenaeus makes his point forcefully by drawing a distinction between the image and likeness of God which was certainly not the intention of the original text. Adam was made at the beginning simply in the image of God, a man; at the end he will have grown also into the likeness of God. (1982, pp. 91-92)

Especially striking about this way of construing "image" and "likeness" is that "likeness" appears to become the superior mode of resemblance to God, in decided contrast to the Priestly tradition. Central to the relationship between ourselves and our Creator, Irenaeus believes, is our bearing a divine likeness by actively assimilating an original resemblance, intentionally turning our lives toward our Creator, whom we do resemble from the first, but only on the basis of God's gracious act of so fashioning us. The fullness of our resemblance to God composes itself gradually within us as we act to bring about what God's Spirit intends for us and helps us to become. For Irenaeus, the image of God in humanity is an original righteousness in the sense of a capacity for right tending that is with us from the beginning. But only in purposively striving to be like God and to obey God's will completely can we truly embody that image. Paradoxically, however, attaining to the likeness of God requires that we have the image of God already within us; we cannot become like God unless we already and always are made in the image of God. But merely bearing certain capacities is not enough to be like God and therefore not enough to fulfill God's intention for us. We must somehow fashion ourselves according to the very image with which God has also fashioned us.

Another way to express the Irenaean view is to say that the divine image, formed in us by an act of divine grace, is the standard by which we are to live, and the divine likeness is that which we become by freely living according to the standard. In psychological terms, Irenaeus's insight is that the divine image in us, which is at once God's image of us, functions as an innate capacity to be like God and to communicate with God, whereas the divine likeness is that capacity activated intentionally in the choices we make and in acting upon those choices. Right choosing and right acting contribute to strengthening in us the further disposition to choose and act. Such a formulation is not wholly dependent on the language of modern psychology. For example, many who followed Irenaeus explicitly, especially the Antiochene writers on Christology of the fourth and fifth centuries came to portray the divine likeness within us increasingly in reference to intention and action, namely in moral terms, especially as a moral righteousness achievable by consistently acting from a sense of internal imperative: human beings bear the divine likeness as they bear in the direction of God's own righteousness, acting always in conformity with God's will. In those whose own bearing is righteous in this sense, God dwells with "good pleasure," and not merely "naturally." Living toward the divine likeness, with Jesus Christ now the paradigm, is humanity's "proper orientation."

One major theological controversy provoked by Irenaeus's view of our created nature has to do with how we are to understand the impact of "the Fall" upon the divine image and likeness in humanity. It is a controversy which, unhappily, is still unresolved. One way to characterize it follows from positing in our created nature an original righteousness (*iustitia originalis*), a mode of being so fully in communion with God that our rational faculties and our freedom are always God-centered. Medieval scholasticism presupposed Irenaeus's distinctions between image and likeness and, in Thomas Aquinas's formulation, expressed original righteousness as the perfection of an actual communion with God that is added to the divine image within us by a special gift (*donum supernaturale*) from our Creator. This state of being in communion with God is the likeness to God that was both lost in the Fall and restored in Christ by way of God's justification (namely, God's pardon) of sinners. Though we have lost our likeness to God through sin, medieval scholasticism maintained, the image of God continues to constitute our humanity as such. From this kind of reasoning, the Roman Catholic position is set out in relatively positive terms: e.g., "In Catholicism the Fall means the loss of something which is not essential to man and does not therefore represent a corruption of his essence" (Niebuhr, 1941).

Protestantism takes a quite different position on the subject. Given the commitment of all the Reformers to the principle that the scriptures are the final arbiter of all theological questions and that there is no exegetical basis for the Irenaean distinction between image and likeness, the actual communion with God that the Scholastics posited in the likeness instead became part of the divine image, and its loss as a result of the Fall strictly entails the loss of the divine image in us as well. Catholicism continues to maintain that the power to sustain our relationship with God is seriously weakened by our sinful condition, but that the divine image in us remains intact, as something like a "formal structural property of human nature" (Pannenberg), or as the potentiality for communion with God (Tillich), or as our essential nature and structure (Niebuhr). Protestantism, however, in bondage to a biblicism run amok, generally holds only that this power, and with it, the divine image in us, has been wholly destroyed. Clearly, dire consequences have followed the specification of an actual communion with God in our original state. (Of course, the Catholic position continues to suffer, with the classical Protestant view, the damages to credibility that accompany *any* notion that "once upon a time" human beings were closer to perfection than they are now.)

Beginning in the nineteenth century, Protestant theologians began to cope with the bleak outlook of their predecessors in a way which, in light of prior rejections of the Irenaean position, is somewhat surprising. Instead of positing the image of God as an original perfection lost by virtue of the consequences of sin, many began to write of a destiny still to be attained, a destiny increasingly conceived in terms of representing God on earth, with the image of God itself becoming a kind of predisposition to attain that proper destiny. So conceived, that image in human beings cannot be lost. Projecting the perfecting of the divine image into a distant future is remarkably reminiscent of the very Irenaean perspective that Protestant theology seemed bent on expunging. Among recent Protestant thinkers, only Barth resisted the efforts to restore at least something of a divine *imago* to humanity. For him, the image of God is not something inhering in human beings, but is rather God's own act of determining humanity to be covenant partners; the divine image that is our promise and destiny is, in Barth's theology, wholly and simply a divine intention.

Another aspect of theological controversy about the image of God and human sinfulness centers upon how we are to understand the freedom to attain our "proper orientation." Prior to Augustine in the late fourth century, theologians maintained that for human beings to achieve a resemblance to God, they must be free to conform themselves to a divine standard itself, often experienced in the form of divine commands. Even though humanity often misuses its God-given capacity for choice, and opts for sin rather than for godliness, the consequences of sinning do not include loss of the capacity for further choice. In this sense, at least something of the divine image in us remains intact even through our sinning. But Augustine's later thinking initiated a change of perspective on human freedom that has unleashed drastic consequences. At the heart of his view was his understanding of the loss of the divine image through sin and the consequent impossibility of living according to the divine likeness. Anselm later expressed this view with special clarity in the prayer with which he opened the *Prosologium:*

"Lord, I acknowledge and I thank thee that thou hast created me in this thine image, in order that I may be mindful of thee, may conceive of thee, and love thee; but that image has been so consumed and wasted away by vices, and obscured by the smoke of wrong-doing, that it cannot achieve that for which it was made, except thou renew it, and create it new."

Further developed in the Protestant Reformation, the position is that all human beings are created in the image of God, but since that image was obliterated as a result of the sin of the first man, we no longer possess the capacity to freely choose to be what God desires us to be, and must remain wholly dependent upon the work of redemptive grace for the restoration of our destroyed divine *imago*. For Calvin, by way of jarring example, such grace must be bestowed on an "elect" predestined to receive it. Those not elected are decreed to be consumed by the consequences not only of their own sins, but of the sins of the whole world in addition. Any resemblance of any human being to God, therefore, is wholly the result of divine agency, and in no way depends upon human activity or response. The cataclysmic consequence of this view has been the burdening of countless numbers of people who in fact are divinely wrought with the soul-destroying feeling of worthlessness at the very center of their being: "And there is no health in us." The only way to fend off such feelings would appear to be through posing as a member of the elect already. As is well known, the Calvinist tradition spawned the thoroughly self-serving idea that material prosperity is a sign of divine favor, rendering to the wealthy and successful of the world considerable advantage over others who also seek to live their lives free from anxiety in the face of its limited duration.

Against this whole line of thought, the Irenaean tradition holds out to us a strong creation faith which will not allow what God has created ever to be overwhelmed completely by the consequences of human sinning. Certainly it is the case that by not tending toward God in all that we do, our being gradually loses its divine likeness. But nothing that we can ever do and nothing that we ever leave undone can destroy the divine image in us, and nothing can compromise finally our God-given power to conform ourselves to that image. "For I am convinced that there is nothing in death or life, in the realm of spirits or superhuman powers, in the world as it is or the world as it shall be, in the forces of the universe, in heights or depths—nothing in all creation that can separate us from the love of God in Christ Jesus our Lord" (Rom 8:38-39 REB). Our created nature remains the source of hope within us, even as our archaic inheritance leaves us without excuse for living as God intends for us to live (cf. Rom 1:20-21).

In the Augustinian tradition, Irenaeus's nonscriptural but nevertheless fruitful distinction between image and likeness devolves into a radical reversal of the heart of biblical faith. The conviction that we share an indestructible image of God borne by the whole of humanity and constitutive of humanity's existence *qua* human gives way to an ineluctable yearning for a paradise irretrievably lost, kept alive in memory only at those moments of bewailing "our manifold sins and wickedness." In countless communities of faith from Augustine's time even to the present, the enormity of the fall rather than the glory of God's creation became the principal subject for proclamation. The archaic foundations of human existence disclosed eloquently in the biblical tradition are lost sight of in the well-cultivated misery that gives birth precisely to what that tradition most ardently abhors: excuses. Were we not all (unwitting) accomplices to the perpetuation of sin, the refrain echoes through the centuries, we surely would be able and willing to serve our God. Dwelling on the sins for which we have been forgiven and the sinfulness from which we have been released, we lose sight of an archaic nature which, in fact, has never been overwhelmed, but only obscured. It is a clear vision of that archaic nature that is so needed in today's pastoral practice, a vision that includes transformation: "Behold, I am making all things new."

The devastation wrought by a deformed Christian anthropology is everywhere present in contemporary attempts at understanding human nature, even and especially in those views that pay no overt attention to the impact the Western theological tradition has had on human self-understanding. Academic psychology, having buried ancient approaches to the *psyche*, looks askance at its "clinical" colleagues for even wanting to visit the cemetery from time to time.

The loss of reverence for soul is compensated by tendentious, mind-numbing volumes purveying the putative "science" of human *behavior*. Psychiatry, hypnotized by precise classifications of "disorders," increases their number while painting an evermore disturbing picture of deepening psychopathology in the population. With its enhanced arsenal of pharmacological approaches to ameliorating mental and emotional distress, psychiatry turns our attention to *soma* and away from *psyche*, and we are left to wonder what could have happened among its practitioners to *Seelsorge*, the care of the soul. Medical "science," with which both psychology and psychiatry scramble to be allied, itself continues to focus on diseases and their ravages, with few clear notions of what the state of at-ease-ness ought to be like for those fortunate enough to recover from their prior affliction by dis-ease. Throughout the mental health professions, the attention given to the scope and depth of disease, disorder, and dysfunction in the human condition is reminiscent of the Augustinian tradition's delineation of the *massa perditionis*, the lump of corruption, that fallen humanity has become.

In the present-day terrain of psychopathology, no mapping of human distresses more amply illustrates the loss of the sense of a divine image that human beings share than that which charts the ravages of abuse and victimization. While many continue to believe that we are winning our current struggle for human dignity and well-being at least in our homes and workplaces, and that oppressors and abusers there soon are to receive their just desserts, it is difficult to see how the desired end of this struggle can be accomplished, given the means we have chosen to employ and the zealousness we have permitted to accompany their utilization. The intensity of the moral outrage that accusations of abuse now elicit provides little solace to, and further exacerbates the pain of, those who suffer it. Surrounded by a great cloud of righteous people whose cries for justice seek the gates of heaven themselves, the abused quickly become mired in their champions' own myriad unresolved personal angers and agendas, unable to extricate themselves from the shroud of an imposed identity that denies them the very dignity their liberators purport to seek for them. No longer human beings who have suffered unjustly certain actions by others at specific times in their lives, while otherwise moving toward horizons of possibility with which it is every human being's task to engage, many abused people become mere "victims," whose feelings, thoughts, choices, and actions are wholly reactive to the assaults of others, real and imagined.

For some "victims," life scales down to a hate-filled scenario of holding fast to long lists of deserved benefices, of blaming others for their disappointments and unhappiness, and of fulminating against the evils of abusive families, employers, men or women in general, corrupt politicians, poverty, social institutions, and global economic cycles, not to mention the easy availability of drugs and the providential order of the universe. Other "victims" turn their rage and indignation upon themselves and get caught in a terrifying downward pull toward self-doubt, self-recrimination, and self-loathing, a demonic condescending that ends inevitably in despondency and shame. Whatever life energy may remain is used up in defending against the specter of death that lurks at the center of self-hate.

Meanwhile, we cling to the illusion that the scales of justice upon which injuries are redressed stand forever balanced. Unhappily, the scales are all too easily tampered with. Allegations of destructive behavior can be regarded as evidence of their occurrence. Professional caregivers must struggle with whether to report accusations that do not appear to them to be plausible. Many anguish over having to make reports when they doubt the advantages of reporting for all parties involved. People who are accused of abuse now seem to have the burden of establishing their innocence, certainly in the "court of public opinion," and frequently in law courts as well, notwithstanding that the rules of the latter are supposed to operate otherwise. Some who are found "not guilty" may in fact be guilty and, tragically, may go on to perpetrate other outrages. But the truly innocent who nevertheless cannot prove that alleged abuses did not occur may face ostracism from family and workplace, public humiliation, and, especially favored today, extortionist demands for "compensation" based upon circuitous reasoning about repairing damage to the soul. When accusations are counted as evidence, and *lex talionis* is the only path to atonement, "discovery" of truth must become a process of covering-over, and there can be no "recovery" for anyone.

Abused persons, persons who suspect or believe that they are victims of abuse, abusers, and persons accused of abusing others all share in common a disturbing spiritual condition: powerful emotions threaten to overwhelm rational processes and responsible decision-making which are part of the divine image in each of us and in all of us together. Preoccupation with abuses suffered obliterates in some victims the perception of abusers as creatures of God even as it raises in others the question of whether the hated abuses might signify at some deep level of being an unworthiness in God's sight. Those who have achieved some small measure of saintliness in their suffering by facile association to the undeserved sufferings of Christ finally falter over the attempt to find any redemptive significance in their pain for anyone else. That there already has been a "full, perfect, and sufficient sacrifice for the sins of the whole world" preempts anyone else's making an atonement out of her and his own victimization. Self-defense against allegations hurled often smothers in the accused the empathy needed for any genuine reconciliation even to be offered, much less accepted. And so, for everyone whose personal identity is held captive by the facticity of abuse, the challenge to become like God, in fellowship with all human beings, is lost by default before it can even be taken up.

*For the first time in several years, **Lettie** has asked for an appointment with her pastor. Earlier, he had helped her through a period of intense turmoil, including a divorce, acquiring new job skills, learning to be sole parent while dealing with rage over her husband's abandoning the family, and finding herself with few friends and no family to count on. To the pastor, Lettie had always seemed impulsive and somewhat volatile, with confusions in her thinking overtaking her when under even modest pressures. Highly judgmental of people who disagreed with or offended her, Lettie was also tactless in expressing her judgments aloud. All in all, Lettie was a very difficult person to work with, and the pastor wondered whether living with her must not border on the impossible.*

When Lettie shared with the pastor some thoughts that her husband had been "shadowing" her in order to get evidence of her unfitness as a mother, and that her husband was planning to have her killed, he reviewed what he knew about the husband and then conjured with the likely conclusion that Lettie's reactions were excessive to the point of being almost paranoid. Other bizarre accounts had an even more delusional quality, so much so that the pastor persuaded Lettie to go to a psychiatrist he would recommend. The psychiatrist diagnosed Lettie as a longtime paranoid schizophrenic. The doctor prescribed and monitored medication, and supported the pastor's further "case management" in the context of a nurturing congregation of persons who knew Lettie and could sympathize with her struggles.

Now, Lettie has come to tell her pastor of some distressing "flashbacks" from her early childhood. Her professor in a psychology class she recently completed suggested to her that she probably was abused as a little girl. Lettie wants to know if it would help her to get into an incest recovery group. With her fragile "ego-boundaries," the pastor thought to himself, and the intense emotional environment of the recovery groups with which he was familiar, it seemed unwise for Lettie to explore her flashbacks, perhaps at all, but at least in such a context. He suggested seeking the advice of the psychiatrist who continued to see Lettie for medication checks, and Lettie agreed to follow through on her own. Later, she returned and reported that the psychiatrist had reservations about Lettie's participation in a recovery group.

In the interim, the pastor reviewed his work with Lettie over the years, and took stock of the quality of their relationship, especially its trust level. Reasonably certain that Lettie would take seriously what he would say to her, and that she would continue to trust him, the pastor ventured to suggest that though she might find relating to people in an incest recovery group a positive experience for her, there would still remain a spiritual problem with which she would have to deal, and that it might be just as helpful for her to deal with it right now. Lettie asked what it could be and listened closely as the pastor asked whether it would be possible for her to forgive whomever had done her harm, no matter what the harm might have been. She said she would have to think about that question some more.

Six weeks later, Lettie dropped by the pastor's office with a considerable amount of news to report. For the first time in over ten years, Lettie said, she visited her mother, now in a nursing home. She took the children with her on the second visit, and all had enjoyed a good time together. More

63

surprising to the pastor was Lettie's account of her efforts to find her father, who had abandoned his family when Lettie was five years old, and who had been reported at various times subsequently to be living on the streets or as a recluse. Lettie tracked him to a decrepit rooming house on the other side of the state, weathered his rage over her intrusion, and with his grudging consent began the process of getting him needed medical treatment and a healthier living arrangement. The pastor is struck with how clearly Lettie is thinking and with how much enrichment she is getting from labors that by themselves seem unpleasant to the point of being repugnant.

(6) CREATED NATURE

In the previous sections of this exposition I have concentrated heavily on the affirmation that human beings exist in the image of God. Now, it is time to deal with the assertion that we have been *created* so to exist, that our very existence is a created existence. "Created" means not only bearing a "whatness" that is conferred, but also a "thisness." Both *what* we are (namely, our essence) and *that* we are at all (our existence) point to a source beyond ourselves.

For the Priestly tradition, we are created in both our essence and our existence out of that primordial chaos, "without form or void," over which Spirit "brooded." Though we are fashioned in God's own image, and have the capacity to conform ourselves to that image as we seek to become more and more like God, we neverthe-less originate from a formless turbulence on which God once acted and continues to act. We have that turbulence as part of our archaic nature. Apart from God's continuing ordering of that turbulence, we can only return to the status of a mere disturbance in a swirl of directionless energy and movement. This is what in the Priestly tradition corresponds to the Yahwist's references to dust and earth out of which we were formed. It is this to which we will return, when the breath of life is drawn out of us. "Earth to earth, ashes to ashes, dust to dust."

As he did with the Priestly tradition's use of "image" and "like-ness," Irenaeus also transformed its entire account of creation from a fetching narrative laden with entrancing metaphors into a puz-zling but fascinating philosophical poem on being and non-being. And from his time forward, Christian thinking about God has included the enigmatic claim that the whole of the created order is a composition of materials themselves created by God out of "nothing." In Irenaeus, the primordial chaos of Genesis 1 is no longer something that merely happens to be without form or purpose; it is quite literally *no* "thing" at all. Initially, Irenaeus emended the Priestly tradition in this way in order to counter alternative interpretations of divine creativity that threatened the credibility of the Christian doctrine of God. Subsequently, his conception of "creation out of nothing" (*creatio ex nihilo*) came to be useful for clarifying the distinctive marks of the Christian perspective to believers as well as to non-believers. More specifically, his formulation helps us to express the meaning of creation faith in the scriptures against views of the God-world relation which were, and are, undermining the foundations of the Christian message.

One such alternative was, and is, a monistic view that holds that God and the world are of one substance, and that creation is only some kind of emanation of the world out of God's own being. The other view, dualism, pictures God in perpetual struggle with coexistent matter over which God has only limited control. In monism, prevalent today in "New Age" religions, the sovereignty of God and the beauty of the world remain supreme, but at a terrible cost to intelligibility in general. In a world pervaded by nothing but the divine, there can be no room for evil and human sinfulness. And yet, evil and sin are everywhere. Dualism takes seriously these phenomena and speaks eloquently to the question of how and why there is unjust suffering in the world. It does so, however, with its own kind of cost to the Christian witness of faith, for its God frequently is overcome, as we are, by the evils against which that God is pitted. Such awareness on our part makes compassion more than obeisance the appropriate focus of our worship, especially at those times in which evil appears to be getting the upper hand. However, a God who is only "a fellow sufferer who understands" (Whitehead) is not the God of Abraham, Isaac, and Jacob, and most certainly not the God who sent his only Son to the cross.

For Irenaeus, the Christian alternative to both views of the God-world relation is anchored in a radical understanding of the nothingness, *nihil,* out of which God creates. In a breathtaking transformation of the Priestly tradition's image of a primordial chaos, Irenaeus asserted that what was in the beginning was not a turbulence yet to be formed but rather *absolute* non-being. The radicality of this formulation is easily missed. For instance, the thinking of his own day had no difficulty referring to *nihil* in the relative terms of possibility and potentiality, of forms ever changing, of *being* that is only not-this and not-that. Instead, Irenaeus requires of us that we take the *nihil* as not anything at all, and in doing so commits us to saying from the outset that this affirmation is also in the strictest sense beyond all our capacities to conceptualize. For Irenaeus, *no* analogies to ways in which human beings create properly applies to understanding the ways in which God is Creator, for example and especially, those that draw on our experience of fashioning something new out of something which already exists in some other form. The "stuff" of which we are made is neither chaos, dust, nor earth, but rather no-thing and nothing at all, non-being in the sense of the absolute other than being. God requires "nothing" in order to bring about the world God intends.

Irenaeus's formulation is not only odd logically; it is profoundly disturbing affectively. For if we are brought out of absolute non-being by God, there must remain much about our existence and nature that can only be impenetrably mysterious. *That* God creates purposively is something we trust has been revealed to us, as has what God desires from us in the created order. What we cannot know is *how* God's purposes are being worked out in creatures whose own substance and structures are, quite literally, no-thing apart from their Creator. In this light, it seems presumptuous of Paul to cite as a matter of knowledge rather than of faith that the Spirit of God "co-operates for good with those who love God and are called according to [God's] purpose" (Rom 8:28 REB). Of particular interest is the impact of his notion on our efforts to comprehend the purposes of unjust evil and suffering in the world. The Irenaean doctrine seems to take away just what many have thought we most need in order to trust that, in spite of the inescapable evils that beset us, God is still God, and God is still good. If we have our origins in "nothing," then there is lacking in us as well as in all created things something intrinsic, whether substance or attributes, to which we can appeal in our efforts to sort out the compatibility of evil, suffering, and human sinfulness with God's creative and ordering activity. The more closely we draw near to the "nature" of what God has set before us in the things of this world, the more threatening becomes the vastness of the *nihil* in which they stand.

From Plato to modern-day personalistic idealism and the immensely popular Rabbi Kushner, dualist understandings of divine creativity have enjoyed a clear advantage over classical Christian thought in helping us make sense out of those examples of evil and suffering that are clearly disproportional to any good that might come from them. Dualism can always appeal to a principle of "resistance" to good ordering that is then claimed to be part of the material structure of being itself, a principle which not even the Cosmic Orderer finally can negate. *Creatio ex nihilo,* however, makes impossible any such appeal. At the center of created being, there is literally nothing to set up a resistance to anything else. And from this Nothing, it is impossible to gain insight into why the some-things of our experience sometimes turn out to be less than we otherwise might wish and expect them to be. Irenaeus's doctrine has made it impossible to "justify the ways of God."

That we cannot justify the ways of God becomes even more frustrating when we face yet another implication of the Irenaean position, that the very conditions and events we feel the need to justify are being called into existence all over again at each and every moment in the ongoing history of the created order. It was Augustine who seemed fully to grasp this aspect of Christian thinking about divine creation. And he relentlessly followed the implications of Irenaeus's understanding to its final conclusion: since the "nothing" from which God created the world has no capacity to be in its own right, creation cannot be only "in the beginning," but, rather, must be continuous. From moment to moment, the created order, with the evils we cannot escape in it, must be a continuing miracle, as nothing has power to persist in being apart from God's ever present creativity. As such, the world and all that is therein has no potency, no agency intrinsic to it. In itself, it is mere nothingness.[8]

Aswirl in these metaphysical clouds is yet another way of dealing with the *nihil* from which we have originated and that in the here and now is deeply embedded in our archaic nature. This is the way of the mystic, for whom confrontation with our own nothingness is but a preparation for our experiencing oneness with the Divine. For the mystic, what prevents us from understanding and achieving oneness with God is precisely our unwillingness to accept the insubstantiality of our own being. By coming to terms with our intrinsic nothingness, the reasoning proceeds, we will grasp and be grasped by "That" which we are already. Mysticism offers to its devotees a variety of methods by which they can achieve, in the midst of the seeming insubstantiality of all things, their true nature as divine. For the mystical tradition, the *nihil* "really" *is* what our word says: nothing at all. Our not "seeing" that this is so is the source of our failure to be what we really are. Hence, it is a profound deception to be told that we originate out of nothing, rather than out of what is Divine.

Certainly it is faithful to Irenaean thinking to take seriously that the absolute non-being from which the world has been created is, in every sense of the term, no-thing and Nothing at all. In moving to the conclusion that we "are" in our oneness with the Divine rather than in our nothingness before God, however, the mystical tradition fails adequately to understand the deepest "reality" of the *nihil*. Now at this level of discourse about Being and Non-Being, as philosophers know well, our very language begins to falter, for it is not finally possible to *say* anything about "what is not" except by appearing to speak about some-*thing* that somehow "is." But this is the kind of paradox that mystics above all others seem especially capable of appreciating. For its adequate expression, I am now going to violate prescribed uses of language and posit a series of negatives that will require close following as well as meditation if they are to do their proper work conveying some of the essentials of Christian understanding.

Rather than that of the mystics, the proper conclusion to be drawn (with the negatives highlighted) about our non-being is something like this: it **cannot** be that the *nihil* is **not** really something we experience, or that it **is** something the experience of which can be finally and completely expunged. The nothingness that we **are** both is and is **not** some-thing which constitutes us. It most certainly is **not** a kind of **no-thing** which makes us transparent in our divinity. What, then, **is** the *nihil* out of which we have come? It **is** that sense of void and emptiness that sometimes comes over all of us and that overtakes and consumes some of us for whole stages of our lives. It **is** the gaping hole felt in the center of the body, the mesmerizing aloneness with only one's own face to gaze upon and not even an echo to distract, the howling abyss opened by the slights of envied others. It **is** the prowling dread that no addiction finally anesthetizes and no scheme for seizing control over life ever conquers. It **is** the Transcendent smirk that belittles self-determination. The *nihil* is that **not**-anything-at-all-ness that plays thief to all our possibilities for **being.**

The *nihil* also **is** the dependency we feel on all the others whom we are not, in relation with whom, and only in relation with whom, we can become who we are. The Priestly tradition put in the mouth of the Creator: "Let *us* make (Adam) in *our* image," and as we have seen, by doing so affirms the gift of relationality at the very center of what it means to be human. We exist alongside and with others, in an encompassing created order that appears both as something merely given and as something for which, together, we bear responsibility before the Creator of the whole. What each of us is individually, or *subject*-ively, is to be worked out interrelationally, in the relationships that sustain us and to which we contribute. The unique possibilities each of us does and does not realize in the process of forming "personal identity" are possibilities for and within relationships.

Confusion about our relational nature is now epidemic in our society. On the one hand, many fail to see that autonomous individuality, their *summum bonum,* is possible only when there is concurrence from those others who otherwise can stand in the way of its achievement. If my autonomy is your subjugation, for instance, or your loneliness, you may decide upon a mode of relating to me within which I will not and cannot ever be truly autonomous.

On the other hand, others lay siege to the principle of relationality in such an assaultive fashion that personal identity is swallowed up in the innumerable forms of "co-dependency" gleefully itemized by their self-proclaimed liberators. But there is no panacea for the dependency that forever stirs within us as human beings. Our relationality is incorrigible and incurable, as is our yearning for an identity shareable in our relationships, a "self" to love in order that we may more genuinely love our neighbors.

Clearly, Irenaeus's transformation of the Priestly tradition leads to interpretations of our origins far beyond the capacity of any in that early tradition to readily imagine. In doing so, however, it accomplishes more than a mere conceptual reformulation of biblical language in the interest of a more abstract and philosophically respectable doctrine of God. By introducing us to the *nihil*, he and the tradition that followed him make it possible for us to see a wide spectrum of human experience as if with new eyes. For, indeed, our archaic nature is a more formidable reality than we may be ready to acknowledge. To borrow judiciously from Hamlet: there are more things in human nature than are dreamt of in our psychologies.

Congruent with the *nihil* out of which we are being created, much of what we are and do seems to be an oscillating between frenetic, reactive movement that resists deliberation and purposive action, and states of inertness, fixation, and fusion that resist change of any kind, even and especially change for the better. Impulsivity points toward the swirling turbulence of the primordial chaos within and between us, and imperviousness stands in the vast formless void which that chaos, in ways beyond our conjuring, also manages to contain. Our individuality, centeredness, and stable relationships must be wrested from a vast natural and social context, which either we must deny, with grandiosity the result, or acknowledge in the awareness of the hovering threats that accompany knowing that we are always, and constitutively, not merely our own. Whether we speak of ourselves in relation to God's shadow, to a primordial chaos, or to the *nihil*, our conclusion must be the same: it is in God alone that, with all else in the created order, we live, move, and have our being, and that we *do* live, move, and have being, together, is wholly a matter of God's gracious opening to us a realm of being, tight against the absolutely nothing at all.

From this vantage point, "created" means, most importantly, being placed and sustained in an environing world not of our own choosing, with a purpose and function determined always in relationship with others and with God's purposes for the whole. And at this vantage point there arises within us inevitably the urge to ask the most fundamental question of all, the question of "Why?" Why did and does God create at all? Why has God created us in and for this particular world? Why should God continue to be "mindful of us," especially since things do not seem to be going as planned in the human sphere? Can the doctrine of created nature serve to answer these ultimate "Why?" questions?

It is tempting to believe so. The very notion that we are creatures open to transcendent creativity at work in all things arouses at least some expectation that we can discover God's intentions for and activity in creating, in the light of which our purpose for being just what we are, in just the kind of world in which we are, might become clearer. We have been told that we matter to the One in whose image we are made, and that our Creator seeks communion with us. Unless, therefore, we are permitted at least to *ask* the "Why?" questions, an otherwise lively trust in God could stagnate, stalled in the middle of ruminations that no amount of disapproval can quell, and earnest searching for God could be abandoned prematurely for the sake of a facile and ultimately soul-destroying agnosticism. How can we *not* ask whether our purpose for being really is, first and foremost, to "subdue the earth"? What could be the "point" of a world needing subduing at all, much less one needing us to subdue it? Indeed, what, after all, is the "point" of *any* conceivable world? For many who have grown world weary, nothingness itself may seem a better prospect to contemplate. Others may long for a paradise that demands nothing from us, and for them the question is, why not a perfect world rather than the one we have? It is not mere idle musing in the name of a wholly abstract philosophy of being to ask "*Why* is there something rather than nothing at all?"

For existential philosophers of this century, these are the questions that express our condition when our existence has become an "issue" for us. In asking such questions, according to these philosophers, we reveal what distinguishes our kind from all other beings in the world: the capacity to sense and to reflect upon the problematic character of our existence even and especially when no answers may be forthcoming at the end of the inquiry. To the Christian understanding of created human nature, however, experiencing our existence as an issue demanding reflection is believed to drive us to genuine self-transcendence, to a way of being that is toward that which both surpasses and confirms us. But self-transcendence is, for finite beings at least, a self-transcend*ing* only, and our raising the questions we must raise about our existence will not be rewarded with the definitive answers we assure ourselves we both want and need. In self-transcending, we must be prepared to let the issue of our existence remain unresolved, because there is nothing within the tradition we affirm that provides a basis for determining answers to any of the "why?" questions about our creation. At best, meditation on the why of our createdness might in rare instances lead some to a new appreciation of antecedent causes. But it cannot open to us the mysterious "why?" of creation at all, because both the mind of the Creator and the *nihil* out of which we are created encompass *us;* we cannot encompass them.

If, then, Christian existence in the world is a tending toward God in the midst of chaos, evanescence, and non-being, and a participating with God in the on-going creation and ordering of things, how shall we truly hope, without illusion, when all hoping both begins and ends with the awareness of our fragility, of our Creator's inscrutableness, of the disappointments that living in a human world not open to God's design makes inescapable, and with the hovering specter of death as the negation of all striving for communion? The unanswerability of this question drives us to reflect once again upon the divine image "in" which we are created. For in that divine image rests the power of reason by which the question can be asked at all. And in that divine image rests the power to decide whether we will trust that what we have heard about our Creator is reliable enough to warrant forming partnerships to tend what has been given us by a gracious God. As existential thinkers have put it, our inability satisfactorily to answer the ultimate "Why?" question about our existence forces upon us a summons to *decide* how we shall live. For Christian faith, the possibility of such deciding is grounded in the divine image which God already is renewing in us, and the decision itself is to live toward God-likeness, receptive to the love with which we are being created anew, and to live with a sense of urgency about sharing such love with others. The self-transcending that God opens to us is to be fulfilled in acts of love rather than through the achievement of comprehension.

Living graciously and gratefully toward our Creator, and lovingly toward everything God has created, is what it means to live according to our ownmost nature, a nature standing in the shadow of God and pulled toward the *nihil* whose "substance" it also "is." In our rare moments of graciousness, gratitude, and love, we are becoming the human beings we are meant to be. For most of us, sadly, these moments are all too infrequent. Indeed, most of the time we do not live as we are meant to. In the striving so to live, however, we can experience more than just glimpses of what life is meant to be in the here and now that God gives us.

PART II
THE GOD WE WANT AND
THE GOD WHO IS

Part One of this project presented a vision shared by both Judaism and Christianity of our nature and destiny as human beings. Central to that vision is the affirmation that, unlike anything else in all creation, we are created to resemble God our Creator for the purpose of representing God on earth. As God's representatives, we are to care for the whole of creation with a tender and loving concern like its Creator's. We can fulfill this daunting responsibility because we possess powers like God's but in proportion to our finite nature. These powers constitute the image of God in us.

Of these several powers, contemporary theologians tend especially to emphasize our *freedom:* the capacity to decide upon and pursue courses of action on the basis of deliberation that considers other actions possible in the situation. The exercise of freedom, however, depends upon another and equally important capacity, our power of *reasoning:* the capacity for discerning and understanding possibilities and actualities, their principles, implications, and limits, and for reflecting upon ourselves in relation to them. Most important, reason makes it possible for us to discern our place and calling in God's scheme of things and to attune our will to God's.

W. W. Meissner, the first of several recent psychoanalytic writers with an interest in religion to whom I will refer in the following pages, expresses this much of the image of God in us as follows:

> The Judeo-Christian tradition emphasizes human intentionality as the peculiar quality by which man is related to divine initiatives and is taken into the economy of salvation. Thus man's is a moral consciousness in which the vicissitudes of intention and choice play themselves out in the drama of spiritual forces. It was by reason of his intellectual capacity, his resources for intentional self-reflectiveness, deliberation, and free choice, that man became the inheritor of the divine right and a participant in the life of grace. By these capacities he was thought able to respond to the divine initiatives

and salvational actions that elevated his spiritual level to the position
of divine sonship. (1984, p. 189)

The very clarity of Meissner's statement heightens awareness
of what it does *not* bring out about the image of God in us.
According to the Priestly tradition, our powers of free choice and
reasoning are given to us by the God who seeks a relationship
with us; they are not innate attributes on the basis of which God
finds us sufficiently interesting to make contact. Further, and
more important, they are linked with still another God-given
capacity, the capacity for *communication* and *communion* with our
Creator and with one another, a capacity that we express most
fully in acts of love. Though we often use our freedom and
reasoning capabilities for our own self-fulfillment, God's intention is that they serve the higher cause of forming and sustaining
loving relationships. The love with which God attends us and that
we are to bestow on others is not possible without awareness,
intentionality, and conscious choice from carefully deliberated
alternatives. It cannot flow from external coercion or internal
compulsion. Whether it is God's or ours, love is always a gift,
thoughtfully rendered, an act of commitment made and honored after weighing and fully accepting the consequences of its
impact upon both the giver and the receiver. The careful reflection that makes love possible is precisely for the sake of such love
and not self-aggrandizement.

It is, then, in our God-given powers for free choice and action,
for reasoning, communicating, uniting, and especially for self-
giving love that we exist in the image of our Creator. As we strive
consciously to exercise these powers in balance, and in partnership
for the care of the created order, we become more and more like
the One who has bestowed them upon us originally. So characterized, the image of God in humanity has been misunderstood in
at least two important ways. One is based upon the premise that the
image represents an original perfection lost as the result of our
earliest ancestors' disobeying God's commands. In addition to the
fact, previously cited, that no credible evidence exists for supposing
the first men and women to be more godlike than those of our own
generation, what also counts heavily against the premise is its

conceptualizing of what humanity is meant to be in terms of a completed state or actualized condition rather than as a destiny yet to be fulfilled. Peculiarly pernicious forms of this first kind of misunderstanding include the view that humanity's divine image was destroyed as a result of "the Fall," and the view that the redemptive work of Christ includes the complete restoration of that image in the here and now (e.g., "instantaneous" and/or "entire" sanctification). The other major misunderstanding of the image of God in humanity is the monistic, "New Age" peroration to the effect that, although appearing to the contrary, we are now what we are intended to be, "really" of the divine substance in finite forms, invited by our Creator and Sustainer to claim our true nature for ourselves. Such a sweet outlook is inevitably overshadowed by the perfidiousness of human destructiveness—from verbal, emotional, physical, and sexual abuse in individual family systems and work-places through "ethnic cleansing" and genocide on national and transnational scales to the destruction of our planet's delicate ecosphere in the service of greed.

The corrective to such misunderstandings is to see ourselves in a God-intended process of growth, striving with God's help and in solidarity with all human beings eventually to become our Creator's faithful representatives on earth. Our destiny will be truly ours when we come to find our greatest joy in caring lovingly for all that God has made. Then, present distresses can become suffused with a sense of hope and a willingness to trust that though things still may not be wholly as they should be, with God's presence and power in our lives we can and will make them better.

With this elaboration of Part One before us, it is time to begin exploring connections between a faith-oriented understanding of human existence in the world and what modern psychology may be willing to say about human beings in relation to God. I believe that the most helpful search for such connections will proceed from examining more closely the origins, dynamics, and goal of the human capacity to love, or in the primary language of faith, our summons to love God and all humankind as we love ourselves. The following discussion is intended as a grounding of the theological outlook just summarized. I hope to show both that the outlook is worthy of assent in its own right and that it conveys considerable wisdom for the practice not only of pastoral counseling but of psychotherapy in general.

(1) FAITH, PSYCHOLOGY, AND THE WELLSPRINGS OF LOVE

The considerations in this section are suggested by two passages from I John: "Everyone who loves is a child of God and knows God, but the unloving know nothing of God, for God is love" (4:7-8); and "he who dwells in love is dwelling in God, and God in him" (4:16 REB). Though the writer seems to confine the scope of the Christian's love to "fellow Christians," his emphasis on love as the essence not only of the Christian life but even of God supports a primary theme of the New Testament witness overall: The Source of our being is One whose eternal nature is to be loving, and our God-appointed purpose is to be loving to all that God loves. John reminds us powerfully that of all the capacities that constitute human beings in the image of God, and even God *as* God, it is loving self-giving that is central. Our freedom and our rationality are worthy of development precisely insofar as they make possible the giving of love out of a sense of deliberation, intention, and choice. But, and here a new issue emerges, if they are necessary to the development of love, they do not by themselves ensure that we will actually become more loving. The kind of communication that freedom, reason, and self-reflection make possible often devolves into self-serving forms. And communion can become mere fusion that swallows up its participants' genuine freedom, and, make loving acts truly impossible. What is it, then, that inspires us to exercise our freedom and rationality in loving ways?

First John 4:19 suggests an answer that at once expresses profound psychological insight and points to the very heart of the Christian witness of faith in the world: "We love because [God] loved us first." The capacity for genuine loving, that is, for actively seeking out and delighting in the well-being of others even when it becomes necessary to sacrifice one's own well-being and perhaps one's very life for others, can become a motivating force only for those who have experienced the reality of being so loved. Only when we know that we matter deeply to someone can we become the kind of person who will let others matter to us. Only when we discover that our worth in others' eyes is conferred upon us in acts of grace and kindness all out of proportion to what we think we may or may not deserve can we so regard others and sacrifice for them. Only when we encounter the steadfastness of another's love can our own love assume that kind of persistence that will make it trustworthy to others. And only when we ourselves have received the cherishing of a loving community can we contribute the kind of love that widens our own communities' spheres of loving influence. It cannot have been a casual statement of Paul to refer to love as the Spirit's greatest *gift*.

But these considerations now force a crucial issue for faith. If, in order for both to become aware of and to make actual our God-given capacity for loving relationships, we must have received love from the very One who calls us to a loving life, how are we to experience for ourselves that love long before even the possibility of returning it can be understood? How do we come to *know* that "God loved us first"? Christian theology's typical answer to such questions expresses the "evidence" for God's love in terms of the sacrifice of Jesus Christ on the cross for the sins of the world, as, for instance, in Romans 5:8, "Christ died for us while we were yet sinners, and that is God's proof of his love towards us" (REB). If we can believe that Christ's death atones for our sins, we apparently will have no difficulty seeing that his death is also *the* relevant evidence for trusting that God loves us. But this approach inevitably will push what little knowledge of a loving God we may have into the abstract, undernourished realm of intellectual assent to the validity of an inferential process. The convincingness of inferences depends too heavily on the impressiveness of their premises and the winsomeness of their manipulators. Intellectual assent to a doctrine of Christ's atonement cannot by itself bring about in us love that is truly imitative of God's. Far more power must be available to us, if we are to sustain

such love in all our relationships across a lifetime, than the inter-
mittent, fluctuating wattage that logic can supply.

Perhaps it was this recognition that convinced the Christian
community that "remembering the Lord Jesus until He returns" is
what is needed to release the energy for replicating the Lord's life
on earth. And, indeed, attending to the story of his "passion,"
hearing it repeatedly in the context of believers' gatherings, and
meditating deeply upon Jesus' suffering and death as disclosures
of his Father's love surely have aroused in countless numbers of the
faithful a sense of the awesomeness of grace, mercy, forgiveness,
and reconciliation with which God lovingly is confronting a world
buried in the craving and the self-loathing that set people at enmity
with each other:

> When I survey the wondrous cross
> on which the Prince of Glory died,
> my richest gain I count but loss,
> and pour contempt on all my pride.
> See, from his head, his hands, his feet,
> sorrow and love flow mingled down.
> Did e'er such love and sorrow meet,
> or thorns compose so rich a crown?
>
> (Isaac Watts)

Even practices such as these, however, do not rise above the level
of believing and passing on what others have remembered. They
cannot by themselves bring about in us an *experience* of God's love
of the sort needed to love others, and the world, in God's own
name. The kind of experience we need is experience that conveys
a powerful sense of acceptance, welcome, approval and affirmation, of enhancing the existence of another, of our own worthiness,
and of having a special place in the scheme of things. Only this kind
of experience can make possible a grateful and enthusiastic participation in all that life offers, even and especially in times of frustration, fear, loss, and suffering. Only this kind of experience can
temper our spirits toward the well-being of others and open the
possibility of a joyful life of self-giving even to the point of self-emptying. The heart of such experience is intimate, nurturing, and

strengthening communication and communion with another who loves us before we are able to love in return.

Stories told and retold, beliefs held, liturgies honored, and meditation practiced all have their roles to play in opening to us the reality of God's love for all humankind. But only the experience of love already bestowed will provide a lasting foundation for the credibility of any belief about the transcendental origin and meaning of such love. Even those beliefs of absolutely indispensable import, recounting what God has done in the life, ministry, death, and resurrection of Jesus confessed to be Christ, presuppose a foundation of love already received, cherished, and shared.

There is little about the content of the previous paragraphs with which psychologically aware readers are likely to have difficulty. Psychological perspectives on love, too, consistently maintain that we can love only as we have been loved. They can accommodate the claim that the experience of being loved requires the activation of a capacity to sense and respond to another's love in the midst of our solitariness, need, dependency, and vulnerability-spawned anxiety. And they can validly promise that with a sufficiency of others' love, there can be activated in us not only the capacity to receive love, but also the capacity to give such love ourselves, in several modes: in return; to others whom we perceive to need and deserve our love; and out of the joy simply of acting on behalf of others' well-being, whether they can or will reciprocate.

The difficulties that accompany all psychological perspectives on love proceed from their claim to say *all* there is to be said about the subject. It is not psychology's positive insights that create problems for human self-understanding; it is psychology's sometimes grandiose attitude of certitude that there are no *other* insights to be had from any other spheres of interested inquiry, particularly faith-inquiry into the possibility of a pure and unbounded love at the center of creation. We may be given reluctant permission to speculate about how such a *concept* of divine love might be generated out of our efforts to make sense of things, but we are led to understand from the outset that any such concept can express only the yearning for a God of love, never the actuality of such a being.

However, unless the Source of love is part of our own archaic nature, psychological hypotheses about the dynamics of love soon bog down in the indefinable middle of a logical regress. If, indeed, only love can beget love, it will require the positing of an indefinite number of generations of humankind in order to identify the acts of love that precipitated the entire succession. As all students of such regressive arguments know, the one thing such chains of reasoning do *not* accomplish is precisely what it is they are set out to accomplish, to explain how something proceeds from something else. An indefinite series in no way leads us to anything that originates it. The love that begets love can hardly be discovered through following out a series of *antecedent* circumstances. Instead, the Source of love in us must be *archaic*, foundational, always and in everyone present, reaching us not from once-upon-a-time, but from "out-ahead."

The most serious difficulty of all with exclusively psychological perspectives on love is their confusion of the *activation* with the *origin* of human beings' capacity to receive and to give love. Certainly, it is reasonable to believe that the human response of love is elicited by human acts of love, that one human being's capacity for loving is stimulated to activity by the loving initiatives of the other(s), and that without love from another, the capacity for love in the human heart remains inert. It is not reasonable to believe, however, that loving action toward another conveys to that other the very capacity to receive the love that is offered. Others' love stimulates our capacity to experience love; it does not create that capacity. While psychological theories may express dissatisfaction with the particular answers that a faith tradition may give to the questions of the originating Source of our capacity to receive and give love, and of how we are to experience that Source, at the end of the day they will be unable to deal with such questions even in principle. What the Christian tradition has to say more explicitly about them is the subject of the next section.

(2) GOD'S FACE AND GOD'S LOVE

The fundamental issue that has come to claim our attention is how we are to experience God's own "pure, unbounded love" in such a way that our capacity for loving in return becomes the active and predominating disposition in and between us. Jesus' parable of the good Shepherd presents an interesting way to pursue the issue further:

> The man who does not enter the sheepfold by the door, but climbs in some other way, is nothing but a thief and a robber. He who enters by the door is the shepherd in charge of the sheep. The doorkeeper admits him, and the sheep hear his voice; he calls his own sheep by name, and leads them out. . . . The sheep follow, because they know his voice. They will not follow a stranger; they will run away from him, because they do not recognize the voice of strangers. (John 10:1-5 REB)

The point of this story, as is well known, is the establishing of Jesus' identity as the trustworthy and self-sacrificing shepherd. For our purposes, however, what is of interest is the anticipation that he will be recognized as such because those whom he intends to "lead out" already have the capacity to understand him, as sheep know their own shepherd's voice. The analogy will bear the weight of application to a new context: as sheep are created capable of knowing which shepherd is their own "good" shepherd, we are created capable of recognizing our own loving Creator, whenever God manifests such love to us.

The parable from the Gospel of John hints that the manner of our understanding who we are in God's sight is analogous to our hearing a trusted voice. Elsewhere in the Scriptures different analogies are more pronounced, based on the symbols of God's *face* and of God's *hands.* For example, and by way of beginning, when Jesus was asked by his disciples about becoming greatest in the kingdom of heaven, he replied by pointing to children and their childlike trust (Matt 18:1-4). Then, perhaps drawing upon a Rabbinic tradition of the time that spoke of angels watching over us continually, Jesus associated the work of angels especially with the well-being of children: "See that you do not despise one of these little ones; I tell you, they have their angels in heaven, who look continually on the face of my heavenly Father" (Matt 18:10 REB). The Jerusalem Bible translators eschew the literalism of referring to the face of God directly and instead render the passage as "their angels in heaven are continually in the presence of my Father in heaven."[1]

Those who may be put off by the anthropomorphism of referring to God's face, of course, may choose to construe "face" as merely a symbol or analogy whose purpose is to make more tangible a perceived vagueness in references to the "presence" of God in human life. When we refer to the face of God, then, we really mean God's presence and, the argument continues, that is what the Bible has really meant all along. Such a narrowing of focus overlooks the deeper, underlying associations in the human experience of God between being in the presence of God, gazing on God's face, and being confirmed in God's love, associations frequently repeated in the Scriptures. A more adequate perspective, which will have direct bearing on how religious experience can be understood from the standpoints of both theology and psychology, begins with the following hypothesis: The face is the *organ* of communicating presence, the primary point of contact between human beings and between human beings and God and the primary medium for communicating love. In the new heaven and new earth, John wrote, all who have remained steadfast in their loyalty to Christ will experience God's immediate presence everlastingly: "They shall see him face to face and bear his name on their foreheads" (Rev 22:4 REB). The face-to-face encounter with God and Christ conveys all the blessings God bestows upon those who persevere in faith against persecutions on earth.

Closely related to the imagery of the face of God are scriptural passages that employ analogies with the *hand*. Psalm 16:11 is especially poignant: "You will show me the path of life; in your presence is the fullness of joy, at your right hand are pleasures for evermore" (REB). Nehemiah speaks of God's gracious hand (or, less literally, "favor") upon him for the rebuilding of the wall of Jerusalem (2:18). And for a later Isaiah, God's hand tenderly and protectively embraces and holds us: "Like a shepherd he will tend his flock and with his arm keep them together; he will carry the lambs in his bosom and lead the ewes to water" (Isa 40:11 REB). Both the face and the hand of God communicate the love with which God intends to surround us all the days of our lives and beyond.

Interestingly, however, there are other and more ominous associations to the hand and face of God in the Scriptures. The hand that protects and bestows also threatens, punishes, and even destroys. Isaiah warns: "So the anger of the LORD is roused against his people, and he has stretched out his hand to strike them down (5:25 REB). Job images God's all-encompassing power in terms of God's hand—"In his hand are the souls of all that live, the spirits of every human being" (12:10 REB)—and cries out for pity, for it is precisely that hand that has struck him down (19:21). The New Testament writer of Hebrews draws on the same analogy to bring to people's attention the dangers of apostasy. Since Christ's sacrifice has brought about the forgiveness of all *past* sins, we are now without excuse for failing to live as God wills. There can be no further sacrifices available to offset sinning after knowing Christ, accepting his saving work, and receiving baptism in his name. It is in this context that the writer says "It is a terrifying thing to fall into the hands of the living God" (10:31 REB).

The same ambivalence evident in the references to the hand of God can be seen in texts that speak of God's face. Exodus 33 contains the Yahwist's understanding of the ambivalence startlingly. Verse 11 speaks longingly of a time when the Lord spoke with Moses "face to face," as one speaks with a friend. But that time is no more: "My face you cannot see, for no mortal may see me and live . . . you will see my back, but my face must not be seen" (33:20, 23 REB). Several New Testament passages carry forward this same notion about seeing God face-to-face. Their consistent meaning coalesces around the conviction that under the conditions of our earthly existence, God does not provide us the opportunity so to encounter him. First Corinthians 13:8 describes our Creator and our future only obscurely, as if through cloudy glass; only in the afterlife can we expect to have God before us unmistakably, face to face. Matthew 5:8 seems to hold that it will be only the pure in heart who shall see God at all. And I John is emphatic to the point of stridency that "God has never been seen by anyone" (4:12 REB).

At Exodus 33:22, however, there occurs a quite remarkable conjoining of references to the hand and the face of God: God's own hand shields Moses from the very face upon which he is prohibited from looking. The same God who has asserted a holy difference and distance between himself and the one whom he has called to lead his people also protects his servant from the consequences both of that difference and of not respecting the distance. Face to face with the Creator, Moses is in danger of being consumed by the awesome and all-encompassing power of God's holiness. Because this is so, he must be shielded if he is to live, and God shields him.

In all these expressions of ambivalent reactions to encountering God, two analogies remain constant: Being in relationship with our Creator is like looking into a sometimes approving, sometimes disapproving face, and like approaching a sometimes beckoning and sometimes threatening outstretched hand. We yearn for God to look with favor upon us, and to hold us in a loving and tender embrace. We fear a look of disinterest, discontent, and disgust, as well as a wave of dismissal or the crush of an angry blow. Of all the passages of scripture that make use of these analogies in order to characterize our actual, our hoped for, and our dreaded relations with God, perhaps none is more powerful than the ancient priestly blessing conveyed by Numbers 6:22-27:

> The LORD said to Moses, 'Say this to Aaron and his sons: These are the words with which you are to bless the Israelites: May the LORD bless you and guard you; may the LORD make his face shine on you and be gracious to you; may the LORD look kindly on you and give you peace. So they are to invoke my name on the Israelites, and I shall bless them.' (REB)

Even the Jerusalem Bible translation, which as we noted earlier avoided the kind of anthropomorphism with which other translations are more comfortable, will not this time shy away from the powerful symbol of God's face bestowing a sense of grace, peace, and safety. Verse 26 is there rendered "May Yahweh uncover his face to you and bring you peace."

Certainly, the Priestly writer is not interested in the symbolism of God's face for its own sake. The more pressing concern is giving expression to God's imparting His *name* to His people. But the tradition this writer helped create nonetheless bears to us imagery of extraordinary import for understanding how our capacity to communicate and have communion with our Creator, given with our creation, is activated by present manifestations of love. The divine love that makes possible the experiencing of life as a blessing, and self-giving in service of others as our destiny, comes to us on the "face" of our Creator in the form of a countenance expressive of approval, solicitude, and even affection. In the act of so gazing upon us, God confers that worthiness, the sense of which is the absolutely indispensable foundation of our loving both God and all that God also loves. We can love neither God nor our neighbors unless we can love ourselves, and we cannot love ourselves unless and until we have experienced being loved, by both our neighbors and by the One who has created all of us for life together.

When the face of God shines upon us, all that we are radiates God's own resplendent glory. We no longer are creatures who merely exist, who merely stand out from both God and the Nothingness out of which God has created everything. Rather, we are filled out with God's own judgment that we are pleasing to our Creator, with a place and a destiny in the larger scheme of creation, capable with our Creator of relishing the good intended for us. At the deepest level of our humanness we "are" that judgment that God has passed upon us. Because God has deemed us so, we "are" creatures worthy of fellowship, together, with our Creator. In place of the all too familiar Cartesian formula, "we think therefore we are," which has dominated modern speculation about what it is to be human, Judaism and Christianity pose a radical alternative: God is mindful of us, and what God "has in mind" regarding us, *that* is what we most fundamentally are; and, we can "see" it on God's face. "On the face of it," when it is *God's* face, there, we are.

As discussed earlier, mysticism sees the *That*, which we are, as God; we "are" the divine substance itself. Instead, the Judaeo-Christian tradition affirms that we are what God sees in us and in turn lets us see in God's face. The image of God that all humanity shares is at once God's image of us, constantly being communicated to us, the source of our self-awareness, self-esteem, self-confidence, and self-giving. Knowledge of how God images us is like the anticipation of seeing on the face of someone who matters significantly to us a look of acknowledgment, affirmation, and delight; and it is like the apprehension we feel that that significant other may give us "the look that kills." The power to fulfill our destiny as God's representatives on earth comes finally from the shining light in the eyes and on the face of our Creator, as our Creator looks graciously upon us. In that "look" is light shining in darkness, peace passing understanding, grace transcending perfidy, hope replacing illusion, vision conquering uncertainty, and love drawing all things into itself.

From these considerations emerge what I believe to be the most important questions with which we must deal if there is to be any rapprochement between faith, theology, and psychology about the meaning of God in human experience. In specific, can the love shining on a *human* face somehow "be" for another also the very face of God? How? Is it not more likely that the love that makes growth possible comes to us *only* on human faces? When we speak of the face of God at all, do we not have in mind simply a particular human face? Are not human faces, after all, *all* there "is" to God? Modern psychology addresses these questions to all for whom faith in and experience of God play an important role in their lives.

In themselves, of course, the questions are not new. They have been raised by philosophers since at least the time of Xenophanes in ancient Greece. They have assumed increasing importance for theologians since the middle of the nineteenth century with Ludwig Feuerbach's attempt to transform the whole of theology into anthropology. From Feuerbach through Nietzsche to Freud and post-Freudian consciousness, serious thinkers continue to confront the possibility, expressed in myriad forms, that "God" is a product of human need and creative imagination, contrived to alleviate the pain of coping with the world as it really is, conjured only in the absence of benevolent human faces in people's lives. Could it be that we create God in our own image, and then deceive ourselves .with the belief that the process is actually the reverse? In the next section, I want to examine closely one recent and impressive psychological outlook for the insights it contributes to dealing with this issue.

(3) OBJECT RELATIONS THEORY AND THE IDEA OF GOD

If a Christian understanding of human existence in the world is to be the orienting perspective for pastoral counseling, we must have good reasons for believing that this orientation is not only coherent and readily applicable, but also that it is congruent with insights into ourselves that modern psychology has to offer. It will be difficult to fulfill this latter expectation without addressing the widely held assumption among psychological researchers and clinicians that God, in the final analysis, is a fiction, however useful some may find the fiction to be for their own purely subjective purposes.

Not everyone, of course, will be convinced that this issue warrants much attention. For example, many Christians dismiss Freudian perspectives on the *psyche* with little more than a wave of a Bible and the incantation of pejoratives such as "humanist" or "atheist." Some believe, still further, that *no* psychological view of human nature should be given any credence, because psychological methods of inquiry are not open to divinely revealed knowledge. (Such persons pose peculiarly difficult challenges in pastoral counseling, especially when they blatantly inform the pastor or counselor that they have come explicitly to avoid "secular" practitioners and want only "spiritual" help.) Others, more knowledgeable about the landscape of current psychotherapies, are willing to dialogue with *some* psychological approaches to religion and faith, but believe that psychoanalysis, at least in its classical form, has long since been supplanted by more effective methods of soul care. For them, both the theoretical assumptions of psychoanalysis and the conclusions drawn from them are out of date. A former colleague of mine, for example, felt that taking Freud and his followers seriously would be "the long way around" to establishing the psychological relevance of Christian affirmations, and that the route could be shortened significantly by juxtaposing with the Christian tradition not Freud but Jung. My colleague persisted in spite of my demur that "God" for Jung is merely a symbolic expression for something that only remotely resembles the God of Christianity. Finally, there are psychotherapists with a psychoanalytic orientation who have a personal interest in religion, and even a deeply personal faith, who nevertheless have concluded early in their studies that psychoanalytic theory and practice thrive on the other side of a chasm simply too wide for religious believers to cross. For such persons, no apologetic of the sort attempted in this section can hope to succeed.

Persuasive as at least some of these views may appear, I do not find any of them convincing. I continue to believe that the integrity of the *psyche* depends heavily on bringing together our unconscious and our conscious functioning. Further, of all theories of the unconscious that modern psychology bequeaths to us, I continue to believe that psychoanalysis has proved to be the most fecund, its early hostility toward religion notwithstanding. Most of the significant inquiries of this century into unconscious functioning have turned out to be further developments of one or more aspects of Freud's own evolving thought on the subject. Thus, I still believe it necessary for the exploration of unconscious processes to begin with Freud, and only then to note how and where departures from Freud seem to be indicated. Within an authentically psychoanalytic framework, it has become possible with integrity to affirm the positive roles religion can and does play in human life. Thus, those who find psychoanalytic theory cognitively and professionally satisfying now can receive illumination rather than debunking of religious belief and practice from at least some of their mentors. And staunch Christians, committed to keeping themselves untainted by alien influences, will find in current psychoanalytic literature more than just a few partners in the quest to understand what a relationship with God can mean.

In the paragraphs to follow, I will elaborate upon the Christian understanding of the image of God with reference to certain recent "object relations" theorists whose work advances considerably the possibility of discussing religion creatively in psychoanalytic terms. I do not intend to undertake a lengthy examination of object relations theory of the sort that aims to advance it to some new level of sophistication or adequacy. In truth, this genre of psychoanalytic reflection is complex enough already. Within it there is a variety of interesting and intriguing difference of opinion that will require years and perhaps decades of further debate among the respective protagonists themselves fully to sort out. In spite of such differences, however, there is a discernible core of convictions that renders coherence to the theory and that, I believe, can be stated clearly and usefully without recourse to undue technicality.

Object relations theory is based upon the assumption that human being and acting in the world have their wellsprings in interactions between people rather than, as Freud and classical psychoanalysts supposed, in intra-psychic conflicts originating in repressed and suppressed biological and psychological drives, wishes, and fears. The word "object" is used to refer, first, to the significant people in our lives who, in our interactions with them, shape who we are. Object *relations* are, first but not finally, the patterns of interaction we form with such persons. Most people's experience includes relations with both "good" and "bad" objects. "Good objects" are those people who affirm and cherish us and who nurture our development caringly, encouragingly, and with enthusiasm. By contrast, "bad objects" are persons who react to us either with indifference, rejection, or persecution, persons for whom we are either a problem or a thing to be manipulated. Often, we carry around with us their hateful projections and we become victims of their emotional and even physical abuse.

Clearly, the availability of good objects is essential to our development as human beings both at the beginning of and throughout life. Equally important, though, but not emphasized equally in object relations theory, is our capacity for *responding* to good objects when they make their appearance. The difference such responsiveness makes to our humanness stands out when we encounter persons for whom responsiveness to others is conspicuously impaired, as in the autistic. Theologically viewed, such responsive capability is given in the divine image we bear, as part of our capacity for communication and communion. Psychologically considered, our capacity for responding to objects as "good" and "bad" is imbedded in unconscious processes by means of which we "construct" the patterns of relating to others that will constitute our uniqueness as well as our humanness. This constructive work yields a variety of representations (which Freud and Jung termed "imagos") of those significant others with whom we enter into relationships. Variously referred to—e.g., as entities, processes, structures, ideational content, images, or schemas in our minds— the representations we construct become our *internal* objects. It is on the basis of these internalized representations more than of the actual features and characteristics of others *as* other that we relate to them and they to us. Our representations—namely, our "internal objects"—mold our sense of what we can expect from and in all relationships; they influence the interpretations we make of others' actions and reactions; and they shape our patterns of giving to and receiving from others.

It can be somewhat unnerving to contemplate that even our earliest experiences of others can be shaped by "seeing" those others in the light of what our unconscious, internalized representations prompt us to see. "Bad" internal objects, such as our representations of people and of our experiences with those whose impact has been negative, may lead us to see not only those to whom our representations correspond, but others still, as worse than they actually are. Similarly, "good" internal objects may lead us to idealize others and even expect perfection from them. Can we learn to see others "objectively"? An affirmative answer will depend on how ready we may be to scrutinize our internal objects and to reassess our representations by letting others disclose themselves on their own terms. Our God-given capacity for loving others as fellow bearers of the Creator's image who share a common calling and destiny will be challenged by ensnarement in a psychologically necessary process of construing others, for a time at least, as mere sources of our own need and drive satisfaction. Happily, it is also in our very nature to strive for more "mature" object relations, despite the obstacles we must overcome to achieve them.

In the "construction" of our object relations, our internalized representations can become congruent with the "real" world to the extent that we become less dependent on others and thus better able to tolerate their being persons in their own right. The more self-sufficient we are, the more open we can become to refashioning our images of others and seeing those others as centers of independent feeling, thinking, and acting; persons of dignity, worth, and need in their own right; creatures bearing the image and love of their Creator. Only when we are willing to affirm the "reality" of the objects external to us on their own terms do genuine *relationships* become possible, in which there is respect, sharing, and mutual self-giving on the basis of what is and can be rather than of what each participant wishes things to be.

Until such maturity is attained, however, reality must continue to be like a word enclosed in quotation marks, for we do not have complete access to ourselves or to the being of another independent of *some* representations that affect our perceptions and judgments about our own selfhood and that of the other. As Rizzuto writes: "We have never experienced life out of the context of objects. . . . There is no representation without object and no object without representation" (Rizzuto, 1979, pp. 77, 83). And: "Real objects . . . are shaped, transformed, exalted, demonified, or deified by our imagination, wishes, and fears" (p. 53). Relationships that matter to us will continue to be influenced by what we want and need ourselves and others to be, both good and bad. None of us will ever be fully free from the patterns of internal object construction we form in earliest childhood. In our neediness, we will construe another as "good" or "bad" for *us,* whatever that other may be like in his or her own right, whatever we may "really" need or not need from the other, and whatever that other may genuinely need and deserve from us. Nevertheless, we can expect to achieve a measure of maturity sufficient to bring at least some of our representation into line with what we discover about the "real" other. Hopefully, we will resist the temptation to bask in our painfully acquired self-sufficiency and objectivity as ends in themselves and, instead, take our delight not only in knowing others better but in giving ourselves for their sakes.

Now, we must return to the notion of good internal objects, for it is here that new approaches to the understanding of God in human experience are emerging in recent psychoanalytic thinking. A word of clarification and qualification is appropriate at the outset of the discussion to follow. The psychoanalytic investigators to whom I will be referring hold diverse views on how we are to understand internal objects and the processes by which we construct them, and I will not attempt to enter into the debates among them regarding which view has the strongest claim to be regarded by the rest of us as normative. For example and especially, it will not matter to the discussion whether internal objects "are" and whether they develop "as" mental representations, memories, thought processes, entities, structures, interactional patterns, schemata, engrams, or some combination of the above. Our inquiry is not about object relations theory per se; it is our image of God and God's image of us from the standpoint of object relations theory broadly but accurately characterized. What *will* matter to our understanding is how the several available delineations of "good" objects together shed light on human beings' experience of God. It should be apparent by now that my own bias is toward those views, such as Kohut's, that emphasize relationality more than self-sufficiency as the proper end both of counseling and of life (self-sufficiency is one important means to the larger end), and that view all our object relations as serving the purpose of anchoring our past, present, and future relationships.

I begin with a premise that has to do with what Meissner calls "an evolving sense of trust, acceptance, and security" (1984, p. 138). Whether this sense is understood as grounding self-identity and self-sufficiency, the capacity for entering into meaningful relationships, or both, what is absolutely indispensable for its emergence and development is a certain quality of care and nurture in infancy, when each human being is vulnerable and helpless. Relevant nurture includes caring not only for the infant's bodily well-being, but also caring for the infant's soul through, again in Meissner's words, "embracing, recognizing, and cherishing." The first "good" object is that person who provides such caring in earliest infancy, the primary caregiver, most frequently the mother. Primary caregivers who are unable or unwilling so to care become their charges' first "bad" objects.

Infants construct their first *internal* objects from both good and bad aspects of the experiences they have of their primary caregivers. No caregiver is capable of being wholly nurturing in the expected ways at the expected times, and will inevitably disappoint, frustrate, and enrage the infant sometimes. However, exposed and unable to care for herself or himself, the infant is prepared to hold on to all the representations of the primary caregiver that sustain his or her need for a "good" object, and to set aside for as long as possible the representations of experiences that were of a frustrating, withholding, or even punitive and destructive character. This pattern is repeated in more complex forms across the life cycle. The danger it presents to our developing relationships can be profound, since our unconscious uses the way we construct our first internal objects as a prototype for all subsequent object representations and relations. One unfortunate consequence is that we can come to expect too much from others and to blame them with a rage all out of proportion to their actual sins of omission and commission.

Although for most infants the primary caregiver is still the biological mother, I think it is misleading to describe the earliest experience of being cared for exclusively in terms of the infant-mother dyad. Accordingly, the next consideration will utilize "parental" language, even though a particular infant's primary caregiver may be someone other than either biological parent. Of primordial significance for early development are two kinds of interaction between parent and child: regarding and holding/being-regarded and being-held. The first dyad is initiated by the parent, but the responsiveness demonstrated by the infant expressed in the second dyad reinforces both positively and negatively parents' further initiatives. "In the beginning," therefore, there is the *inter*-action. Similarly, from the beginning, regard is central to holding: regarding *is* a way of holding, and being-re-garded is crucial to the experience of being held.

In a quite literal sense, regarding/holding and being re-garded/being held take place "face to face." It is on the face of the parent that the infant sees himself/herself for the first time, hope-fully as a subject not merely of gazing, but also of the other's interest, regard, care, protection, hopes, commitment, and cove-nant. But, painful as it is to acknowledge, some infants will be consigned to seeing themselves as merely a source for the other's contentment or misery, or as something somehow contemptible, or as if adrift in a sea of cravings from which there will be no relief. What is being described here is what object relations theorists call the "mirroring" relation. Victoria Hamilton succinctly expresses its heart:

> The first image or outline to which the human infant orientates visually is the human face. Normally, the infant further selects out the face of the mother. As he comes to familiarise himself with its contours, what does he find there? The mother's face reflects how she sees her baby. This reflection may mirror either the baby's or the mother's own feelings and mood or, optimally, the interaction or overlap between these two. (1982, p. 113)

For Hamilton, as for Winnicott earlier (1967), what the child sees in the parent's face, as if in a mirror, is also the parent's image of the child—how the parent sees, feels about, and judges the child; what the parent wishes and hopes for not only in the child, but also for the relationship that is beginning between them.

One prevalent but problematic way of construing what takes place in the mirroring between infant and parent is to see in the encounters the *imparting* by the parent of the infant's constitutive sense of worthiness. Upon this view, "good enough" parents create for their children both the bonds of a nurturing/nurtured relation-ship and communicate that essential worthiness the sense of which will make it possible for them eventually to become loving persons themselves. In this kind of thinking, people who turn out incapable of maintaining their part of loving relationships are merely victims of either neglectful or abusive parenting early in life, who need and deserve "corrective emotional experiences" promised in re-parenting modes of therapy.

Another, and better, understanding of mirroring comes about by looking closely at what "good enough" parents are *discovering* about the child and themselves in the process of expressing their adoration: that their own lives are being summoned to share in new creation, and that the creature who is coming to be will have her or his own contribution to make to a scheme of things far grander than those that human parents could ever devise. On the face of such parents is wonder, gratitude, confidence, patience, hopefulness, steadfastness, all suffused with love perceptive of the loveliness, lovableness, and lovedness of the child. An essential support for such a countenance, however, is the child's smiling encouragement and confirmation that what parents' faces show is the result of their "seeing" correctly what, in fact, is there to be seen. Lacking experience of benign mirroring, and lacking positive reinforcement for benign mirroring given, some people come to need a form of therapy that can help them discover for, and in themselves, what a parental figure and/or their own children may have been unable or unwilling to see in them.

Object relations theorists do not seem to pay sufficient attention to the role that an infant's capacity for *noticing* plays in the mirroring relationship. The exercise of that capacity is essential for the interaction of regarding and being-regarded to be complete. Regard that goes unnoticed is ineffectual. To be sure, many infants go through childhood eager for regard that seems never, or at least, only intermittently, to come. For some of these deprived children, rage over frustrated cravings may attain levels impossible for anyone ever to satisfy. Others may simply extinguish expectation altogether and then communicate an indifference that discourages the recalcitrant parent from genuine caregiving when the impulse to offer it finally strikes. But still other infants seem not to notice their parents' ministrations sufficiently, making it that much more difficult for the parents to sustain consistent caregiving.

In all of these instances, the infant's capacity for noticing is *activated* by, but it is not *created* in, the experience of being regarded. And even when the capacity is activated, we cannot be certain that a particular infant will *exercise* the power to allow herself or himself to be regarded, held, nurtured, and inspired. A loving face may shine brightly upon the infant's, but the infant may let it go unnoticed. In theological language, the freedom both to exercise and not to exercise any of our God-given capacities is part of the gift of our humanness. However agonizing it may be to others when someone chooses not to do what would enhance a relationship, it is nevertheless just such freedom that enables us to transcend merely reacting to others and to achieve genuine *inter*-acting. Inter-action is a choice for interdependency over co-dependency and love over compulsion.[2]

Enough has been said on the mirroring relationship as interactional. It is important also to understand the mirroring relationship as *transitional*. This notion opens up an array of interesting discoveries about the role of transitional experience in the formation of our idea of God, and the role of the idea of God in our other developing object relations. A way into the discussion is provided by Meissner: "Religion partakes of the character of transitional phenomena or the transitional process and as such achieves its psychological reality and its psychic vitality in the potential space of illusory experience" (pp. 177-78).

"Transitional" here refers to serving the ends of what psychoanalytic thinkers believe is life's most important transition, from infantile dependency to mature self-sufficiency and reciprocal relationships (in contrast, for instance, to some religious believers' conviction that the transition from this life to the next is what truly counts). Transition in the psychoanalytic sense requires gradual separation from the "holding" environment that supports us in our vulnerability and helplessness; formation of a reflective inner self capable of giving to as well as receiving from others; and organization of life around plans, goals, and values that include at the very least socialization, work, play, intimacy, generativity, and devotion. Intense anxiety accompanies this transition at every phase and stage of the life cycle. It is tempting to cling to the security provided by a known though limited environment rather than to become the persons we are meant to be by enduring the pain of letting go the comfortable and venturing into the unknown, either by themselves or with new and untested companions. However, there are available to us sources of comfort and strength in our growth anxiety that, without eliminating the anxiety altogether, can quell its more debilitating effects. Object relations theorists refer to these sources of comfort and strength variously—for example, as objects, representations, states of consciousness, relationships, experiences, modes of experience, and phenomena in general—but always use the term "transitional" as a modifier. In order to simplify the exposition, I will refer to transitional *objects* in the paragraphs to follow.

As "transitional," transitional objects have both a particular function to perform and a particular kind of meaning in the unconscious. Their function is to provide soothing in situations of high separation anxiety, and their meaning is their symbolic representation of our earliest sources of nurture, comfort, and strength in times of vulnerability and helplessness. A frayed and tattered piece of blanket, a teddy bear, or a soft doll are the kinds of early transitional objects we cling to in the absence of the holding provided by a primary caregiver, and we permit objects of these sorts to represent (namely, to make present) the painfully missed caregiver in the stressful here and now. In shifting our affections to transitional objects when the people they represent are absent, we learn to comfort and strengthen ourselves, and, by so doing, make some of our first moves away from dependency.

We might conclude from these sorts of examples that all our relations with transitional objects are dominated by illusion, by how we want things to be rather than by how things really are. But such a conclusion would oversimplify things considerably. While we normally outgrow the transitional objects that comforted us in childhood (for instance, Winnie the Pooh went on the shelf when Christopher Robin went off to school), we never outgrow our need for what they provide. The "potential space of illusory experience" is an unusual and alluring kind of "place" for creative activity of a high order, a place we continue to visit long after we have left our childhood behind. What is unusual about it as a place is that it is a place *between* the external world and our inner life, between the realms of object and subject, illusion and reality. Here, the creative impulses of the human spirit flow spontaneously. Great works of art and philosophy abound in profusion, along with enchanting myths, stories, dreams, and visions. It is something like the prophesied "Holy City, new Jerusalem, coming down out of heaven from God" (Rev 21:2 REB), a purifying habitat appearing in the first moments we magically transform our favorite things into the much loved persons from whom we derive our greatest comfort and strength. In the transitional object—whether a scruffy toy or a complex of skyscrapers, a lullaby or a symphony, a bedtime story or a Pulitzer prize-winning novel—those for whom our hearts long become wondrously and genuinely here; they "hear" for us. Their hearing us renews us to face the challenges of change. Though we gain access to this peculiar kind of life space by means of imagination and play, what we create there will vehemently resist being dismissed as "mere" fantasy.

The things of the playroom and the toybox are but prototypes of later, more "mature" transitional objects that constitute every normal adult's world. Because the transition to maturity is a life-long process, we will always experience pain in separating from those who matter to us, even though we know that there will come a time when we must take our leave from them and they from us. But the very capacity God has given us to reason about things is also the capacity to keep the things of our experience together (namely, to *sym-bolize* them) by representing (re-presenting) them in wondrously varied ways. Symbols bring near to us secure sources of nurture and courage for facing the challenges of the unknown. Little can be more calamitous to the human spirit than failure to let things in experience stand for and make present caring persons when they are much needed but not available. Such failures are in the truest sense of the word, *dia-bolic;* they keep separated and alienated what cries out to be connected. Only the "real" other is allowed to count, and in the absence of that other, those afflicted with such a limited and limiting perspective remain caught in an undertow of craving that neither outrage, envy, nor feigned grandiosity and self-sufficiency can overcome.

As we grow toward and through adulthood "normally," we gradually replace the soothers and encouragers of our early years with others more empowering of adult development. Pastimes, friends, hobbies, mentors, work, sports, lovers, the arts, and even religion can serve important transitional needs as well as other functions. Of course, any of these may become fixations that inhibit further development, as can other transitional objects, however pleasurable or necessary they also may seem at the time: for instance, food, gadgets, alcohol, sleep, fast cars, multiple sex partners, and legal and illegal drugs. God also exhibits features remarkably like those of transitional objects, as we now will see.

The first psychoanalytic thinkers uniformly followed Freud's highly negative and polemical pathologizing of religion that reduced religious acts to the status of obsessions and compulsions, and religious beliefs to fantasies that prevent people from coming to terms adequately with how things really are. The idea of God itself, Freud maintained, is a neurotically twisted representation of a cosmic father figure left over from each young boy's earthly struggles to eliminate his own father from competition for the affections of his mother. Divinizing the father helps to make possible relinquishing the struggle and moving on to more mature expressions of sexual development. When worship of the fantasized God is itself relinquished, Freud preached, humankind's proper business of attaining a responsible and realistic outlook on life can proceed without further intrusions.

Many recent object relations theorists have come to see the role of religion, and more specifically, of belief in God, quite differently. Rizzuto believes it possible to chart "the secret, unconscious weaving of images, feelings, and ideation which converge in the childhood process of elaborating a representation of God" (1979, p. ix). With others, she construes this process as one that begins early in the pre-oedipal rather than in the oedipal period, draws upon images of the mother even more than of the father, involves female as well as male children, and persists throughout life instead of ending in the period of latency. Though both real parents and wished-for parents contribute to each child's early images of God (p. 44), the images themselves involve creative processes in the unconscious mind that are not bound totally by the raw material received.[3] Our earliest ideas of God will be tied to memories, which later will fade, of our first nurturers' keeping us comfortable in our small part of the universe. When we no longer think and speak as children, we will compose an idea of God capable of containing and expressing a new kind of yearning altogether, now for the unseen Creator and Sustainer of the whole of things.

The process of constructing a God "representation," and of shaping other object relations partly by means of it, continues through life and greatly assists our maturation, so long as we reassess each representation along with all our other object representations that make up the fabric of interpersonal existence:

> The key object relational contribution lies in its perspective that an "object"—in our case, the personal god concept or representation—is not merely a *product* of psychological development, but also *enters into relationship* with and promotes the development of the self. (Spero, 1992, p. 72)

Rizzuto is optimistic about the prospects of reassessing our God-representations in the interest of more adequate object relations in general: "Those who are capable of mature religious belief renew their God representation to make it compatible with their emotional, conscious, and unconscious situation, as well as with their cognitive and object-related development" (p. 46). While there exist in abundance representations of God that are immature, developmentally arrested, retarding, illogical, parochial, heretical, and even psychotic; there is nothing superficial, transient, chaotic, neurotic, or psychotic about the process itself by which such representations are formed and transformed. By locating "God" in the illusory space of transitional objects in general, object relations theory offers an intriguing framework within the parameters of psychological method for affirming God as a constituent part of the human universe.

As do all representations of significant others in our lives, our representations of God draw upon a profound array, first, of memories. Rizzuto (p. 56) believes that visceral, sensorimotor, proprioceptive, eidetic, perceptual, iconic, and conceptual memories of primary object relations are all blended in the unconscious process of forming a God-object. While her technical language may seem forbidding, her main point is readily comprehensible: Our God-representations draw to themselves a rich panoply of other images, feelings, thoughts, and wishes. In kinship with all our transitional objects, these representations nurture in us an openness to the sources and power of being in and beyond the world, a sense of personal identity that persists through the many and sometimes frightening changes we feel taking place within us as we move through life, and a sense of togetherness with others in a trustworthy world filled with real and potential companions.

The God of our faith reassures us that at finitude's center there is a conscious, caring presence to whom we and all things forever matter: "Love never ends." As we venture onto new and uncharted terrain—whether geographic, intra-psychic, interpersonal, or valuational—our God is the One upon whom we depend when anxiety threatens to overwhelm our confidence and our sense of hope. Our God is the One who extends over the whole course of life a trustworthy promise to hold us fast and never abandon us. This is that One whose intentions for us far exceed all that we can either ask or think, whose expectations are always tempered by patience and grace, whose name can be expressed as "I Will Be There."

The substance out of which children begin, very early in life, to compose for themselves such a comforting, sustaining, encouraging, and encompassing idea of God, is parental countenance, the expressions on their faces by which parents gently communicate to their children what life is and can be like. Hopefully, what will show on parents' faces consistently is the kind of confidence about life and its possibilities that will arouse in each infant an abiding level of trust. If their children choose to catch such a vision and make it their own, then throughout all their lives their anxieties can give way to feelings of security, their frustrations can become challenges rather than calamities, the pain of absence can become the opportunity to create cherished memories, and reaching out to the benevolent faces of those who love them will be only the beginning of a process that intends the embrace of all creation. Infants so blessed are able to gather up their experiences of benign, powerful, parental regard and weave them into the rich texture of an image of God and of themselves gazing upon the face of that God without fear, savoring God's kindly face perpetually shining with grace and peace. And they can take comfort and strength from God's own gracious hand while "taking a hand" at living to the fullest themselves. The infant whose use of his own hand Winnicott saw as a bold move toward self-pacification and separation from the mother's breast also was discovering what the hand of God is for, and the meaning it has for becoming what truly loving parents want their children to be above all else: creatures who can "handle" life on their own.

(4) GOD IN OUR IMAGE?

Whatever we may conceive to be the ultimate *aim* of human development, modern psychologies influenced by psychoanalytic method and thought strongly affirm that what is of fundamental importance to achieving it is the quality of caring we receive from others, especially in infancy but throughout life as well. Our attitudes toward and beliefs about life and the world are profoundly shaped by those who genuinely care for us and who help us both to care for ourselves and to become caring of others. The images we form and inwardly cherish of our caregivers comfort and strengthen us especially at times of struggle with new challenges when they are absent. Our images of those others contain their images of us, and it is from these latter that we compose much of our own self-image and self-understanding. Our ideas of God, to which we attach many different sorts of memories, thoughts, and feelings, are formed and reformed from images of those significant others. They function to assure us that our relations in and with the whole of things will have the same qualities, whether benign or malignant, that we have found in our other relationships.

Modern psychologies that fell under the sway of Freud and the most politically correct of his followers bequeathed to their successors a theory of the human psyche which, though finding only pathology in humankind's religions, nevertheless and ironically championed the cause of scientific rationalism with an enthusiasm bordering on religious zealotry. Nevertheless, the very method for which we must remain indebteded to Freud has transcended many of the narrow doctrines Freud himself gleaned from it, including his somber assessment of the importance of religion in human life. Freud's God-idea contained only the detritus of religions that have failed to mature according to their own standards, and the religious expressions he criticized have long been denounced by the prophets and priests of those very religions. By contrast, the God-representation that has emerged in at least some quarters of object relations theory is of One who is the preeminent embodiment of that kind of love that alone grounds a proper directing of our distinctively human capacities and actions. This is a God who at every stage of our life-journey aligns Her or Him"self" with our highest and noblest efforts to achieve a self/personhood genuinely capable of revering and rendering service to others and to all being.

Belief in God, then, no longer can be summarily dismissed as an inhibitor to growth, and for this advancement of psychological understanding, object relations theory deserves commendation. The major obstacle the theory presents, from a theological point of view, is that it persists in addressing the question of God in human experience only at the level of concepts or representations that exist in the psyche alongside all the other object representations we form as we grow toward maturity. Rizzuto, for example, unequivocally and proudly declares that her book (its title to the contrary notwithstanding), *The Birth of the Living God*, is not about God at all, but is about object relations per se. Meissner suggests no way beyond this circumscription of faith's God, and Jones, in his otherwise fascinating proposal to substitute "internalized patterns of relating" for "internal objects," seems content to leave human bonds with the sacred reduced to "expressions of a person's internalized affective relationships" (Jones, 1991, p. 110).

Moshe Spero (1992) worries that "God" in object relations theory will remain, as did Freud's "God," nothing *but* an idea, representation, or internal object. Spero's concern is pertinent. Once we have enumerated the functions and meaning of our ideas of God on the basis of analogies with transitional objects, is there anything *more* to be said about them? At first glance, Spero's approach to the problem seems to chart a way for psychology to allow itself to be transformed by the transcendental perspective of religion and the experience of faith. He insists that we need "some method for schematizing veridical object representations of God, a representation not confused with other types of representations that are modeled upon interpersonal relationships" (Spero, 1992, p. xv). And he faults psychoanalytic thinking for having no model that is both theoretically sound and clinically sophisticated by which what patients say about their God as objectively real can be responded to directly, without changing its content into the "psychological view of the image of God as a product of representational dynamics" (p. 49). His point reformulated in more explicitly theological terms, Spero seems to believe that object relations theory does not really get us beyond Feuerbach, who in the nineteenth century dangled before the trembling faces of all who would make Christianity respectable in the Age of Enlightenment a heretofore unspeakable proposition:

> The necessary turning-point of history is therefore the open confession that the consciousness of God is nothing else than the consciousness of the species; that man can and should raise himself only above the limits of his individuality, and not above the laws, the positive essential conditions of his species; that there is no other essence which man can think, dream of, or imagine, feel, believe in, wish for, love and adore as the *absolute,* than the essence of human nature itself. (Feuerbach, 1957, p. 276)

Against this nothing else tradition, Spero muses on the possibility of "veridical perceptions or intuitions of God" (p. 48) and reaches the end of his exploration looking for, in addition to our concrete object representations of God, "deep preconceptions on the order of an 'archaic heritage' that disposes the psyche toward God's presence" (p. 142). He suggests that in psychotic experiences such preconceptions might better be discovered, for "the psychotic's unconventionality often seems to yield special access to an enviably real, sensual, luminous, and palpable godlike dimension beyond human consciousness" (p. 81). Spero seems to want to confront Freud's atheism on Freud's own ground by discovering a real rather than fantasized God somewhere in our primordial experience of the world.

Some may be tempted to follow Spero's pursuit of pre-oedipal experience to the threshold of an encounter with God unmediated by any representation whatever. I believe, however, that such effort is unnecessary and even quixotic. Psychology has much to offer when it delves into the structure and dynamics of those capacities that make us the distinctive human beings God has created us to be. Faith and theology speak eloquently to the larger issue of the origin of these capacities, an issue that cannot be dealt with adequately within psychology alone. When each discipline tries to do the work of the other by itself, it compromises the integrity of its own methodology and yields mixed and often unsatisfactory results.

In our experience of God, perception and intuition surely are involved. To the extent that they are involved, to that extent Spero's quest is pertinent. But *what* is it that our perception and our intuition lead us to "see" when we step onto holy ground? The very method of inquiry to which Spero is committed inevitably generates precisely the kind of answer he appears not to want: in experiencing God, what we "see" are the loving faces of those we count on to care for and about us. When we acknowledge God in those faces, far more is happening, contrary to Spero's supposition, than mere perception or intuition can account for. One way of expressing what is happening is that we are *inferring* the presence of something that we do not experience directly. Medieval scholasticism and the "natural theologies" that follow in its train have argued persuasively that we are dependent far more on inference than on perception for our knowledge of God our Creator. The more psychological way of stating this point is in the terms that give Spero difficulty: seeing God in a caregiver's face is "seeing-*as*," *construing* something experienced as "really" that *and* something else besides.

109

I believe that there are fewer difficulties here than Spero seems to believe, and that the best way to dissolve the difficulties is to continue concentrating on the analogies between our ideas of God and our transitional objects. One of the most important things we learn from experience with transitional objects is that the world that is "there" for us encompasses possibilities beyond both the spatio-temporal continuum of empirical reality *and* the construc-tions of our own imaginations freed from empirical constraints altogether. Transitional objects do not "live" simply on one side or the other of Freud's narrowly defined dichotomies of pleasure principle/reality principle, illusion/realistic possibility, appear-ance/reality, or wish fulfillment/truth. They have their being, value, and power both between and beyond all such dichotomies. They are neither fact nor fancy; they are both and more. What is true of all transitional objects is quintessentially true of our God representations and of the world coherence we experience by means of them. What we affirm about God is neither an "objec-tively" valid representation of a real but transcendent entity, nor is it a complex of wish-driven abstractions formed in our minds out of other internal object representations and encounters with "real" objects in an empirical, interpersonal world. It is both, inseparably.[4]

Another important aspect of the analogies between transitional objects and our ideas of God has to do with the "presence" that transitional objects mediate. I have repeatedly complicated the exposition of this point by alluding, through hyphenated expres-sions, to the complexity and the profundity of the process of representation. Here, I will attempt to make explicit the basis of the hyphenating. Our greatest misunderstandings of the process of representation arise when we confine the meaning of "repre-sent" merely to letting something stand for something else. In this context, the signifier we select brings something to mind that in some important sense has been and is *absent*. For the moment, it takes the place of whatever we intend for it to represent. Words for things, by way of example, make possible the experience of at least some of those things "vicariously."

There is a deeper level of communication possible between human beings than that of signifying. At this level, "represent" means to make present again (re-present), or better, to allow something to make itself present to us. The "representation" is a *re-presenter.* Among theologians, it is common to distinguish these two levels of representation in terms of "sign" and "symbol." Signs are conventional designations that merely stand in the place of something. Symbols possess both power to make that something present and a quality of transparency through which what it represents can make itself present to us. It is as if the symbol clears a way for what it symbolizes to come to us. Thus, symbols offer us a closeness to things divine that signs cannot. Literalism extinguishes communication with God, whereas symbolism enlivens it.

By way of illustrating concretely these somewhat abstract considerations of signs and symbols, I offer an easily recognizable item in Christian communities of faith, the wedding ring. On the surface, liturgies that give attention to the ring indicate that in the formal language of the churches, there is the same confusion about signs and symbols as persists in our ordinary language. The wedding ring is referred to indiscriminately as a "sign," "token," "pledge," *and* "symbol." At a deeper level of meaning, however, important distinctions are expressed subtly and beautifully. Traditional services assign to the minister words along the lines of: "The wedding ring is the outward and visible sign of an inward and spiritual grace, signifying to all the uniting of this man and woman in holy matrimony. . . . " The blessing of the ring(s) is in the form of a petition that the wearer(s) will abide in peace and in God's favor. In the exchange, the ring seals the giver's pledge of fidelity and love. Though the words used revolve around what the wedding ring *signifies* (stands for), the meaning of the words clearly is *symbolic.* The rings will make present continually in the lives of their wearers the blessing and expectations of their church, their mutual pledges of commitment to each other, and God's own interest in their future together. Several contemporary liturgies make explicit use of the term "symbol"—couples exchanging rings refer to them as symbols rather than as signs—and in one tradition the rings are spoken of as signifying to the community of faith "the union between Jesus Christ and his Church." Clearly, the wedding ring is enveloped in a variety of assigned, conventional meanings. But it also bears deep aspirations and power that couples and their surrounding faith communities both confer *and* sense. One hint of the symbolic significance borne by the wedding ring is the range of feelings typically generated by taking it off, for whatever purpose. However eager we may be to split the "conferring" and the "sensing" in the interest of determining the object's "objective" and "subjective" meaning and function, it will resist our efforts at such control.

Transitional objects are symbols in this sense. The presence which they mediate is palpable, but it is neither wholly "objective" nor wholly "subjective." In our use of transitional objects, we allow ourselves to feel as if in the presence of caring, supportive others "in" the symbol. Such an understanding of "presence" calls radically into question presumptuous distinctions between what is "out there" and what is "inside us," between realms of fact and realms of meaning and value, between the contents of consciousness and the content of dreams, between what we see before us and what we hope for. For four hundred years now, Western philosophers have engaged in erudite but unproductive disputes about how to deal with such a dualistically schematized world, in which God, too, is reduced to the status of *either* an object or a subject. Instead of continuing the search for a "real" God out-there and a "true" representation of that God in-us, we can more profitably dwell on what and who our God-representations, like all transitional objects, make *present* to us.

Our image of God, as well as our understanding of God's image of us, are contributed to by our "internal objects," the representations we form of those who have loved us and love us still. But our internal objects are more than just raw material for putting a pleasing face on how things work. In those images as well as on the faces of those they represent, we also experience the very presence of God, in a "place" that is neither wholly outside nor inside us, real or fantasized. The images of loving faces that we carry with us and the God-representations we fashion from them are our most important symbols of all: They make God present to us.

The notion of the "real presence" of something spiritual in the material things of concrete experience is carefully articulated in the language of theology, but is virtually unknown in many sub-systems of modern psychology. In theological reflection, "real presence" is perhaps most frequently discussed in reference to the Church's sacraments, especially the sacrament of the Mass or Eucharist. All Christians are asked to believe that in the celebration of the Eucharist, the crucified and risen Lord is genuinely in the midst of the gathered congregation, as those authorized to do so distribute consecrated wine and/or bread and as worshipers remember gratefully Jesus' life, passion, death, and glorification. Though there are differences of opinion among Christians over *how* Jesus becomes present in the eucharistic celebration (e.g., through bread and wine changing their substance at the hands of the celebrant; through the faithfulness of the congregation's remembering the Lord; through Christ's graciously fulfilling his promise to be with his followers, and so on), beneath these differences Christians "with one accord" proclaim *that* Jesus is present, and that his presence is part of the fundamental mystery (*mysterion*) of the faith: "Christ has died; Christ is risen; Christ will come again."

There is a great deal happening in every eucharistic celebration. "Elements" fit for the divine host to occupy are gathered and dedicated. In receiving just these elements, worshipers affirm their power to be in the presence of Christ (even if they also believe that their priest's initial transformation of the elements in no way depends upon their own faith). Mysteriously, God-in-Christ joins his followers as they consume what they have dedicated to the purpose of bearing and containing him. On their way to maturity as disciples, Christ's people are receiving not only their priests' blessing, but Christ's own transforming grace for the arduous journey. Further, "angels, archangels and the whole company of heaven" and all the faithful who have preceded this generation are mystically in communion with those now meeting around the table of the risen Christ. The "medicine of immortality" is joyfully received, as this horizon of earthly existence opens toward a transfigured life with Christ and all the "saints" in worlds without end. In all that is happening by means of them, the eucharistic symbols pulsate with power derived both from the community of faith that

113

makes careful use of them *and* from the One for whom the symbols stand, who has promised to be present in power in them.

Other events of "real presence" abound in the life of faith, and involve in the same ways as does eucharistic worship the power of symbols, their users, and all that they symbolize together to forge a communion between human beings and the Divine: dreams and visions, Scripture shared reverently, celebrations at sacred spaces and times, prayer and meditation, sacraments, and devotion to icons, to name just a few. For Christians, the preeminent symbol is conveyed in the multitude of images of Jesus Christ, "the Word made flesh," "in whom the complete being of the Godhead dwells." All of these symbols "make present" our most important Source of comfort and strength in times of anxious change, in the manner of other transitional objects. But by looking especially at transitional objects central to the life of faith communities, we can discover a dimension to transitional experience in general that object relations theories often miss. Our symbols from the life of faith do the work they are supposed to do because the love they convey originates from the God whom they ultimately represent. And all transitional objects do their appointed work because, in the love on the faces of those they commemorate, there also shines love everlasting, "love divine, all loves excelling."

A final reflection on the analogies between transitional objects and our ideas of God: Encounters with caring persons, and the relationships with them that transitional objects make possible, themselves are profoundly symbolic. As we have learned, transitional objects help us to sustain a sense of the presence of other caring creatures who with us bear God's image. In this way, they aid us in maintaining relationships. From the perspective of faith, being held and nurtured by someone who loves us as unconditionally as human beings are capable of loving is itself a representation of our most archaic (namely, origin-ating) relationship of all, being held and nurtured by the One who even now is creating us and calling us to fulfill our destiny. This suggests that one purpose for all our finite relationships is to prepare us for a loving relationship with God. And indeed, for faith, the most important transition in all of life does involve detaching our loyalties and affections from the things of this world, even from those who mediate the love of God to us, in order that we can devote them to their proper "object." As Martin Luther wrote: "Let goods and kindred go, this mortal life also . . . God's truth abideth still." This need not mean turning our backs on those who have loved us. Our task is, rather, to turn toward the One for whose sake they have loved us. And correlatively, genuine love of others supports their own leave-taking from us in order to love God with all *their* heart, soul, mind, and strength.

*No sooner than they had gotten their marriage off the ground, the "second time around" for both **Carl** and **Sandy,** their relationship seemed headed toward rock bottom. Sandy's teaching contract was not renewed; her son was arrested for drug possession; and Carl was terminated from a sales position soon after he completed a protracted and debilitating treatment for cancer. Though the tumor appeared first in a lung, his doctors assured him that it had been caught early, and that the prognosis was encouraging. Much as they loved each other, the couple despairingly told their pastor, **Lucie,** the pressures on their marriage seemed more than they could handle. By remaining available and supportive over the next few months, and by mobilizing several kinds of support that parishioners were only too willing to provide, Lucie helped Carl and Sandy stabilize their marriage and apply their newfound energies to getting new jobs, seeing Sandy's son through some of his early adolescent crises, and even becoming involved with some of the church's outreach ministries. A year later, Sandy gave birth to the couple's first child together.*

Another year passed, and Lucie was transferred to a church two communities removed from Carl and Sandy. Soon after beginning her new appointment, she was walking to her car across the church parking lot when she saw Carl sitting in the front seat of his parked car, weeping. Lucie helped him back to her office, shocked to hear his urgent plea, "I need you to show me how to die." Carl's cancer had returned, was invading vital organs, and according to his doctors would claim his life in a matter of weeks. Carl proceeded to tell Lucie that things had never been better for him at work or at home, that Sandy and her son both were completely attuned to him and his needs, and that his young daughter was bringing joy into his life. Expecting a great deal of anger from Carl, Lucie was somewhat unprepared to hear him reiterate needing help in dying: "I'm not going to have a chance at being successful in life, but maybe I can die like a man." Not knowing just what this phrase might mean to Carl, she nevertheless agreed to give him whatever time he might need in the days and weeks ahead. She next visited Carl in his home, with Sandy and her son and their daughter present, and with the family's blessing Lucie agreed to see Carl individually from that time on.

Though Carl subsequently expressed to the pastor a degree of anger over being "cheated" out of a full life, his principal concern was how fearful he was of what death held out to him. To her gently phrased questions, Carl shared a long and anguished history of family relations gone sour. An only child, Carl spent his first few years with an alcoholic, fun-loving, desperately insecure mother who was regularly beaten and subsequently abandoned by Carl's father. By the time Carl was nine, his mother had gone through two other marriages and numerous affairs, finally "running off with a drifter," to the denunciation of her whole family for being "no good." On the first day of high school, Carl received the news from the aunt who had taken him in that his mother had been murdered by someone she had "shacked up with" the previous night. He remembered fighting back tears of anger and of shame, and of asking no further questions about his mother's whereabouts, the murder, or the disposal of her body. He felt it important from that time on to make something of himself that somehow would make up for his mother's "wickedness." He lived with a disabling feeling that his mother was burning in hell for her sins, and that, as her son, he could all too easily fall into hell with her.

Carl's condition deteriorated steadily over the next three weeks, and though he had grown more accepting of what was happening to him, his fears of what lay beyond death for him seemed not to have lessened. On a bitterly cold evening, Carl sat by the fire in his den and with a sense of wonder told his pastor of the dream he had had shortly before she arrived:

"I was standing on a shore, looking out into blackness, feeling waves on a lake lap my feet. I knew I had to walk out into the water, but all I could see in front of me was a mist and moonlight behind the clouds. Then, the mist seemed to lift a little, and I could see a shoreline on the other side, not too far to reach. Halfway across, it seemed like there were some people waiting for me on the shore. But I didn't know them."

Lucie asked Carl to look again, closely, at the people. With considerable effort, he seemed to bring the gathering before his eyes. Then he gasped: "My mother is there, looking at me!"

Softly, Lucie asked, "What do you see on her face?"

"She's smiling; she's happy," Carl replied, tears streaming down his face. "Do you think it's time, Lucie?" he asked the pastor.

"Carl, I think maybe it is."

Two days later, Sandy called Lucie to tell her that Carl was in the hospital, "tied up in tubes." When Lucie entered the hospital room, Carl's eyes were open. Smiling, he beckoned her to come close and listen to something. Lucie bent over Carl, and with great effort he told her that he had been looking at his mother's face again and again. When Lucie asked Carl how he felt when he did that, Carl replied, "My mother's face turned into God's." A few hours from Christmas morning, Carl died, at peace.

PART III
THEOLOGY IN
PASTORAL COUNSELING:
THE DIFFERENCE IT MAKES

The major theme of this book is that faith and theology play the foundational role in pastoral counseling and have much to contribute to psychotherapeutic practices as well. In the pages to follow, the focus will be upon the positive differences that theological understanding can make to pastoral interventions. I believe that it will enhance appreciation of these differences if I begin the discussion with a brief review of two venerable but highly problematic ways of integrating theology with pastoral practice. As we will see, they bear an uncanny resemblance to ways in which contemporary psychiatric models of mental disorders intrude upon the practice of psychotherapy.

(1) SOME DIFFERENCES THEOLOGY HAS MADE

In the history of pastoral ministry, theology has made its influence felt in two especially troublesome ways. The first is by *articulating and imposing a rigorous structure of religious and moral expectations and prohibitions in the service of ecclesiastical hierarchies seeking to extend control over not only their parishioners, but over secular society as well.* The sacramental system of the high Middle Ages is especially illuminative of this approach. Pastoral care and counseling revolved increasingly around confession, penance, and absolution, through interventions prescribed in advance by manuals prepared explicitly to shape the work of unreflective priests in the confessional. It is more than mildly disconcerting to compare many of these documents with the Diagnostic and Statistical Manuals of Mental Disorders promulgated over the past forty years by the American Psychiatric Association.

Both genres aim at precise diagnoses for the sake of focused treatment. However, many of the manuals for confessors substituted a process of impersonally dispensed penance for the deeper conversations that might have furthered parishioners' spiritual growth beyond relief from guilt. And the latest psychiatric handbook, DSM-IV, similarly enamored with taxonomy, is hard put to make convincing its claim that "clinical judgment" is indispensable

121

to the handbook's application in the concrete. Many confessors' manuals gave away the Christian vision of human beings' bearing God's image to ever more detailed classifications of sins and the prescriptions for healing them. Correspondingly, DSM-IV's creators are bewitched by computer searches of literature, data analysis and re-analysis, and carefully monitored field trials in the interest of "unbiased" information about mental disorders. Its editors claim that their revised descriptions of the soul's pathology are all in the interest of strict empiricism and "clinical utility." Not so subtly disguised in their concern for objectivity, replicability, and conceptual precision is their eager anticipation of DSM-IV's *economic* utility as well. DSM-IV deftly anticipates the questions of insurance adjusters skilled at avoiding paying their insurees' treatment bills. The manual seems bent on smothering insurers' niggardliness with the pseudo-certainties of a new *gnosis*. In addition, therapists of all persuasions will easily salivate over the introduction of many new mental disorders justifying treatment. Not surprisingly, far more are added than eliminated, and the new manual promises even more on the horizon. In the not too distant future, there may be at least one "mental disorder" for each of us, and the psychiatricization of the human community will be complete.

There are eerie similarities between the abuses of the sacramental system in the Middle Ages and the form modern psychiatric practice seems to be taking, at least if manuals for diagnosis are any indication. Both confessors and therapists craft systems enabling them to achieve maximum power and control over those whom they purport to serve. Their systems define with unassailable finality each person's place in the universe of sin, mental health, and disorder and they channel enormous resources to whomever their respective guilds certify to deserve them. Fees, whether for indulgences or for therapy, are ingenious devices for denigrating human beings' bumbling efforts at maintaining wellness and striving for wholeness on their own.

The other way theology has influenced pastoral practice is by *formulating learned definitions of faith and spirituality and imposing them upon the faithful without regard for the myriad ways in which human beings, whether within or beyond the churches, actually experience, believe in, and communicate with God.* Typically, what theology deduces to be pleasing to God includes commitment to a particular set of beliefs and worship practices, adherence to a prescribed set of behaviors, and, sometimes, the cultivation of particular religious experiences (e.g., dreams and visions, baptism in the Spirit, stigmata, healing, speaking in tongues, and so on). Those with the requisite theological acumen and ecclesiastical power quickly fall prey to an arrogance that sees everyone else at less advanced stages of pilgrimage toward that more complete spirituality whose contours only the wise and the powerful can know fully. Theology knows best, even though God's Word, Spirit, and very being may actually be working in others beyond the parameters of the normative theology of the time.

There are disturbing analogies between this employment of theology in pastoral practice and the struggles for sovereignty over the mental health professions waged by the most ardent in the various "schools" treating distressed persons. Staunch advocates of a particular psychology of human nature and experience will allow only those therapeutic interventions that the respective theory can justify, irrespective of their clients' real needs. Psychoanalytic true believers doggedly track their patients' distresses to their intrapsychic "foundations," as if the external world were merely a presupposition to be noted casually and in passing. Jungians eagerly absorb all of life's smaller problems into the one overarching, inescapable, intimidating, and everlasting problem of individuation. Rogerians (perhaps, like Taoists, on the verge of extinction) exude empathy inexhaustibly, all the while scorning interpretation as tantamount to assault. Gestalt therapists' here and now fetish threatens to sacrifice their patients' histories at the altar of solipsism. Therapists who have given fealty to the American Association of Marital and Family Therapy accept without demur the group's conferral of freedom to practice from any theoretical orientation as long as it is "systemic" in nature. Cognitivists torque warped thinking; re-decisionists retrofit decision making; and behaviorists dissolve mind and soul altogether. And most insidiously of all, Health Maintenance Organizations dismiss with the wave of a check any and all therapies that assume a time frame at variance with those determined by the canon of profit. Only brief therapies are funded; now, alone, is the hour for cure.

If the only kinds of difference theology can make to pastoral care and counseling are those described in the previous paragraphs, it is not difficult to understand why pastors and pastoral counselors might be reluctant to incorporate theological reflection into their helping strategies. And, indeed, they *must* protest vigorously any arbitrarily imposed ordering of human life as inimical to their caring for persons whose relation to God unfolds in significant measure on God's own terms. But so also must pastors and pastoral counselors resist the tendency to idealize modern psychology's articulations of the human condition. As Part Two made plain, depending for a theoretical orientation on the psychological sciences alone will not lead to a sufficiently comprehensive framework for pastoral counseling. Uncritical application of *any* psychological orientation will lead to the kind of intrusions into caregiving that *a priori* psychological commitments invariably generate. The responsible alternative to a theology that harms spiritual growth hardly can be the latest and most popular psychological fad. Instead, what is called for is an understanding of human distresses and possibilities by means of a theology that is faithful to God rather than subservient to ecclesiastical causes and hierarchies. I hope that Part One has expressed adequately just such an understanding, and Part Two has shown how theological reflection can proceed in sustained dialogue with modern psychology, to the benefit of all who see both disciplines contributing to the care of souls.

We should now be in a position to see the positive differences theology *can* make to pastoral counseling. In the discussions to follow, I will present case material from the ministries of conscientious pastors and pastoral counselors with whom I have been privileged to work, in a context of theological reflection on the kind of caregiving each case or cluster of cases represents. In my judgment, the situations that lead people to seek pastoral counseling always have been primarily crisis-oriented, and typically are situations in which their distress is related to significant loss. Accordingly, I will devote a portion of this part of the project to issues of *crisis management and grief resolution* in the practice of pastoral counseling. I will then turn to an area of profound disturbance in the human psyche that pervades a wide array of symptoms and disorders today: *the experience of shame*. All too many people today are struggling to make their way in a demanding and unforgiving world burdened with feelings of unworthiness in the depths of their souls. Ostensibly to cope less ineffectively with the everyday, many disguise to others and to themselves these debilitating feelings by a variety of ruses—drivenness, addiction, dependency, abusiveness, eating disorders,and criminality, to name only a few. In doing so, they run the risk of losing sight altogether of who they truly are: bearers of the divine image who share a common calling and destiny. Tragically, others soon become blind to the divine image in them also. I will conclude this book with an examination of how pastoral counseling can address the shame-filled with the eyes of faith.

(2) IN CRISES WITHOUT END, AMEN

Whatever else may be the responsibilities and interests of busy pastors and pastoral counselors, those whom they serve expect them to be available and effective in situational crises of many kinds—such as illness, marriages, accidents, moral decisions, family conflicts, hospitalizations, job losses, births, divorces, assaults, questions about the faith, deaths, new opportunities, and re-marriages— to name only a few. For this reason, training in crisis intervention is especially valuable to pastoral care and counseling in today's church and world, so much so that it has become tempting to frame all pastoral work with distressed persons in terms of crisis-response. Crisis methods include a range of interventions that typically are brief, focused, and within the range of the typical pastor's competence and experience: e.g., establishing trust quickly; empathically responding to feelings; formulating the precipitating problem simply and accurately; identifying what decisions are possible in the circumstances; guiding the choice of an appropriate course of action; and encouraging new learning from resolving the particular crisis at hand. Such an approach minimizes the risk that pastoral actions might inadvertently bring about harm, and it prescribes referral to more adequately trained colleagues for whatever longer term therapy may be indicated once a particular crisis has passed. Crisis training has become to the present generation of pastoral caregivers what Rogerian, "client-centered" training was to their immediate predecessors.

Crisis methods fit nicely the busy schedules of caregivers who carry a multitude of responsibilities. They expedite quick solutions to problems, making it possible for the helper to move on to others in need, confident that the effects of the work just concluded can endure. Sooner rather than later, however, every pastor and pastoral counselor will be challenged by people whose crises are but the most recent in lives hounded by one calamity after another, whose torment has overwhelmed most who have offered them care in the past, and whose future looks to be nothing but dreary repetition of by now familiar misery.

*In the first week of her new pastoral assignment, **Sheila** met **Joy** and her husband, **Harry,** in the frozen food aisle of the local grocery store. Harry appeared eager to tell the young pastor of their interest in joining the church, and invited her to come by their home for a visit. Joy said very little during the brief exchange, but nodded approvingly at Harry's invitation. Late that afternoon, Sheila pulled up to the couple's trailer, which had a forlorn look about it and was sitting just a stone's throw from the town dump. The small lot was strewn with rubbish and items that seemed to belong inside, and at the rear of the trailer a car sat with its hood up, surrounded by miscellaneous engine parts.*

Two preschool age children ran out to Sheila, and with great effort spoke words that she interpreted as "Periwinkle is dead." Harry beckoned to her, and she entered a front room that was crowded with toys, odds and ends of dirty clothes, dishes caked with food scraps, and broken pieces of furniture. Joy was in the couple's bedroom, holding a small, lifeless puppy. Her face showed the signs of much crying, but as Sheila studied her face, Joy appeared to her almost trance-like. Another puppy began licking Sheila's shoe, and Joy began to tell how the children had recently found them, abandoned and hungry, near the dump.

What followed was a brief visit that disclosed that the family had recently moved to the area to be near Joy's newly widowed sister, that Harry was finding enough odd jobs around town to feed the family, and that Joy has been feeling "mopey and down in the mouth" for a very long time. Sheila found in Joy a considerable shyness as well as sadness, but noticed that during the visit Joy had found a way to seat herself very close to Sheila and to stay close. At the end of the time together, Joy walked Sheila to her car.

The next day, Joy telephoned to thank Sheila for the visit. She expressed loneliness and wondered if they had done the right thing moving away from other family members and friends. She had named the other puppy "Dandelion," but feared that since her first puppy bearing the name of a flower had died, she ought to change this one's name before it cursed her, too. Thinking for a moment, Sheila chose to volunteer the name "Hope." Joy seemed almost delighted with the suggestion.

In the middle of the night, Harry called the parsonage, distraught that Hope had become sick and looked as if she were going to die, and that Joy couldn't stop crying and shaking. Fearing that the puppy's death, particularly since bearing the new name, Hope, might throw Joy into an even deeper crisis, Sheila chose to go to the couple's trailer and stay the night. The next morning, she took the puppy to a veterinarian thirty miles away, received assurances of the animal's generally sturdy constitution, and returned Hope to the family, along with a handful of medications that would further ensure Hope's speedy recovery. Sheila hoped that the check she had written the veterinarian would clear. Joy later telephoned to say that the children had played with the medicine vials and that some of the pills were lost.

After joining the church with Harry the next Sunday, Joy embarked on a series of volunteer efforts in the congregation that kept her in closer proximity to Sheila than at times the pastor found comfortable. Nevertheless, Sheila felt it important to encourage the efforts, and found satisfaction in Joy's opening up to her more. Joy asked Sheila's permission to hug her, told her pastor that she loved her more than she has loved anyone outside her family, and regularly sent notes and little handmade gifts. Harry thanked Sheila profusely for "putting some spunk back" in his wife. Other laypersons reported to Sheila that Joy was intrusive and ill-tempered with them, and were wondering how to deal with her.

Toward the end of the first year of Sheila's pastorate at the church, Joy sat tearfully in Sheila's car and said that she had missed out on everything God wanted her to do with her life, that her marriage had been a mistake, that she was not a fit mother, and that she could see nothing ahead for her

127

but feeling worthless to everyone. Sheila sensed anger in Joy's voice, but Joy would not give it form by attaching it to any particular lamentation. Joy's outburst took Sheila by surprise, so much so that she had nothing to offer except a listening ear into which Joy poured more of her long-standing misery.

Her new litany of woes included a yearning in adolescence to become a nun, subsequent rejection by the Order, marrying Harry out of a need to be loved, feeling forced against her will to have children, molestation by an uncle in early childhood, and a rape on the night of her graduation from high school. Joy's first sign of acknowledged anger took the form of a bitter tone to the words, "I've never been able to please my mother, no matter how hard I've tried." In her speechlessness, Sheila was aware that she felt Joy was angry with her, but had no idea of what she might have done to provoke it or of how to get Joy to talk about it. Later, alone in the parsonage, Sheila realized how angry she was feeling toward Joy and struggled to find its source.

Sheila had looked forward eagerly to welcoming Joy and Harry into her congregation, and initially had found in Joy's neediness a way to fulfill her desire for more excitement in her ministry through more intense helping relationships. By not anticipating just how needy and demanding Joy would turn out to be, Sheila now finds herself with more "excitement" than she bargained for, and feels caught in Joy's dependency without knowing how she managed to fall into it in the first place. Fortunately, Sheila also recognizes that it is time to step back, reconsider what is happening within herself, and find a way to let her feelings guide her to reclaim her pastoral responsibilities to Joy.

Sheila admits that she has allowed herself to be manipulated and subsequently betrayed by Joy, whose omnivorous needs have seriously depleted her energy and enthusiasm for ministry. Once an overflowing fountain of gratitude and admiration, Joy has become demanding, irritable, petulant, and with some of her special caregivers almost hostile. Harry seems to need Joy more than she needs him, perhaps for the excitement she brings to his life, and so he eagerly stays on an emotional roller coaster with her. Others in Joy's life, however, are craving an end to the chaos. But just when Joy's demands threaten to drive her caregivers in the church away (and by doing so, offer to them at least some temporary relief), her sadness makes a timely reappearance, along with her litanies of victimization, that seduce others to re-invest themselves, convinced that this time Joy will "get it together." But Sheila now knows better, and the knowledge is very disturbing to her. The disarray of Joy's trailer and yard are poignant symbols of the disarray of Joy's soul. Her name mocks her spiritual condition, and Sheila is losing hope that Joy's life will ever get better.

From at least as early as her adolescent years, Joy's life has been a collage of unstable relationships, poor self-image, and emotional volatility. Her crises cry out for a variety of interventions beyond those that Sheila and her congregation have so far provided. DSM-IV will insist that for Joy to break out of the cycles of turmoil that have dogged her for decades, she will need not only the supportive, crisis-oriented care of her church, but long-term, intensive individual and group psychotherapy, short-term hospitalizations for the times she is likely to become actively suicidal, and medications for the psychotic episodes that to this point Harry has successfully kept hidden. It may be that only long-term hospitalization and residential treatment can provide Joy the optimal setting to work out the changes she must find a way to make in herself. With all of these interventions, extending perhaps over as many as five to ten years, Joy's future could be brighter than her prospects now appear.

If the interventions I have just enumerated are the *only* keys to Joy's liberation, then she and those who care about her really do have little to be hopeful about. Given the limited resources Harry and Joy have available to them, psychiatric interventions of this scope are about as likely as an expedition to the top of Mount Everest to strengthen Joy's cardiac output. However, at least until providers can be found who are prepared to treat Joy for little or no compensation, there *is* help available for her of a sort that may be the most cogent help anyone could offer her anyway.

The members of Sheila's congregation who continue to hope, albeit futilely, that somehow and someday Joy may "get it together" nonetheless have perceived correctly a core issue in her life: her lack of structure, boundaries, and limits, and her need for help in holding things together within herself and in her family relations. Joy's condition is indeed chronic, and she will need patient attending over a long period of time by caregivers capable of relinquishing expectations that their modeling of a structured approach to life will "take" right away and that Joy will be functioning on her own soon. Eventually, these expectations may be fulfilled, but certainly *not* in the immediate future. The long view and not the short run must become the source of hope that energizes Joy's caregivers. Taking the long view can engender precisely the kind of hope that is the single most important ingredient in any therapy that Joy will ever receive: the unwillingness on the part of caregivers even to consider the possibility that she might *not* get better. The expectation that Joy *will* get better can provide her the kind of "mirroring" most needed in the growing and healing process.

Can Sheila help members of her congregation prepare themselves for the "long haul?" For this is the most important work she may be able to accomplish on Joy's behalf. The image Sheila currently has of Joy is of a desperately lonely, fearful, clinging, and manipulative young woman who is driving her parishioners to distraction wondering whether there is any end in sight to the caregiving she seems to demand. When Sheila recovers that part of her own psyche that she has let drift into the turbulence of Joy's psyche (her own desire to be cared for and appreciated), and when she has regained enough of her wits about her once again to understand that pouring herself out for another is a risky tactic for winning that other's genuine regard, she will be better able to see Joy as a person in her own right and not demand her to be the exuberant and delighted recipient of her own need to minister at deep levels. Then, Sheila will be in a position to bring her image of Joy more into line with God's own image at this particular point in Joy's life.

Joy's God-given capacities for weighing possibilities; for deciding how she will act on behalf of both herself and others; for shaping her life in accord with standards to which she will remain faithful even when it proves costly to do so; for entering into and sustaining relationships in which there is mutual affection, trust, and honest communication; and for devoting herself to all that truly is worth her devotedness are all contorted into self-serving by long-standing feelings of deprivation, anger, and anxiety. Their exercise is contaminated by her near hopeless yearning for faces filled with compassion, hope, affirmation, and commitment. For Sheila and her congregation, the task is to offer just such faces, on whose countenance Joy can see the loving face of her Creator. With God's countenance lifted toward her, Joy can begin to share rather than hoard her capablities and to receive her greatest "joy" serving the Lord with gladness by helping others to believe in themselves as God's own. Can this happen to Joy? It can as long as she remains surrounded by those who believe in their own hearts that this is indeed the future that God envisions for her and that, because it is, they themselves have no choice but to strive patiently as well as confrontationally to help Joy believe it also.

Some parishioners seem to have an uncanny capacity to draw caregivers into the maelstrom of their own incapacitation, no matter how competent, mature, and well-trained their helpers may be. In attemping to minister to Joy, Sheila and members of her congregation repeatedly found themselves awash in Joy's emotional binges and vulnerability. They falsely consoled themselves with the fantasy that Joy was about to put her life together and that all she needed was just a little more help. Since Joy had so little grasp of the divine image "in" her, it was not difficult for those who cared about her to lose sight of it also and as a result to find themselves maneuvered into managing one crisis after another, convinced that without their help, Joy would go under. In the second case I want to discuss, the lure to attack crises one by one is of a different sort.

*Roger has been a leader in his church for several years. He diligently seeks his pastor's advice on "spiritual matters," and he witnesses frequently to the congregation through his leadership, his strong belief in all that the church stands for. He and his wife, **Sue,** have been thought to have the ideal marriage. His pastor now is deeply troubled. What slowly has come to his attention has made him wonder whether Roger is indeed the kind of Christian he was believing him to be.*

The first of the pastor's many surprises occurred following services one Sunday when Sue, in a tear-filled conversation, poured out her anguish that she was facing damnation because she could not have children. Roger had told her in no uncertain terms of "what the Bible says" about this matter:

131

Women's salvation is through the bearing of children. Sue believed she had no right to question her husband as the spiritual head of their household and had taken Roger's pronouncement as if it were indeed the Word of the Lord. When she expressed her desire to begin adoption proceedings, Roger became adamant that only Sue's bearing "his" children herself could suffice and that, soon, God would make this possible. At that time, Sue and Roger had been married for over twelve years, and both were approaching their forties. When the pastor later conversed with Roger about the biblical passage in question, Roger confessed, winsomely, that what was really at stake for him was not his wife's acceptability in the sight of God but his own sense of manhood. He admitted that he felt less of a man that he "couldn't get his wife pregnant," and that he could not accept the idea of raising "some other man's child." Then, he expressed anger at Sue's desire for a child and called it being disloyal to him. Roger bitterly said that he should be enough to satisfy Sue. In further conversations with Sue, the pastor saw clearly that she felt she had no right even to explore the possibility of adoption without Roger's wholehearted support.

While discussing the childlessness issue with the couple, the pastor began receiving reports from other members of the congregation that for some time Roger had been spending time with certain women in the church. While Roger said that his efforts were in the direction of helping these women become "more spiritual," his friends began to feel that more was going on than mere spiritual guidance. Roger then came to his pastor to confess that he had a serious gambling problem, that it had kept him out several nights a week for many years, and that it had resulted in a string of recent losses he was having difficulty covering. Appearing to be genuinely contrite, Roger asked whether the Bible explicitly condemned gambling as a sin, and then asked the pastor to pray with him for release from bondage to the temptation.

Three months later, the pastor was shocked to hear that Roger had staged a rigged poker game with several parishioners, and had won enough to stave off foreclosure on his house and repossession of his car. Wanting to confront Roger with his swindle, the pastor found himself distracted by the agitation in Roger's voice during a telephone conversation in which Roger pleaded for guidance about his behavior with several women. He told his pastor that he wanted to learn how to overcome his persistent urge to "play mind games" with women to see "how far he could go" with them. Roger seemed to be overcome with feelings of guilt and shame, and his desperation inspired the pastor to promise to work with him and guide him toward effectively controlling his impulses to manipulate women.

*Over the next few months, Roger seemed to be progressing well. Then, the pastor received undeniable confirmation that Roger had initiated several extramarital affairs over the past several years, and that his most recent affair had just occurred with a young woman who also loved gambling and with whom he had taken several trips to participate in high stakes poker marathons. Roger's absences at work led to his being fired from his job. Roger told the pastor that the supervisor was a new man in the company who fired him in order to replace him with a relative. While the pastor, ever hopeful about his ability to intervene successfully in Roger's sin-abounding life pondered what he should do next, Sue telephoned him to tell of a meeting with "the other woman," who ostensibly told her "the whole story" as background for her demand that Sue divorce Roger. Sue asked the pastor to meet with her and **Delia** together, outside of Roger's presence, to help both of them to deal with issues of adultery, divorce, and remarriage. The pastor insisted that if such a meeting were to be held, Roger must attend also. Reluctantly, Sue agreed. With no small amount of trepidation, the pastor arranged a time for all the parties to meet with him.*

At the meeting, Sue shared her anger toward Roger, but reaffirmed her conviction that divorce was not an option for her. Roger poured out a painful acknowledgment of his infidelities and general unworthiness, ending with his asking for a temporary separation in order to allow him fully to "atone" for his sins. Delia sat passively, and said only that since Sue did not now have Roger, she should free him for someone else. The pastor continued to visit with Roger and Sue during the period of their separation and encouraged the congregation to surround the couple with Christlike love while they worked to rebuild their marriage.

Four members who withdrew their memberships from the church during this time later told the pastor that while Roger was living apart from Sue he had swindled them out of thousands of dollars in a dishonest investment scheme.

Happily, today's besieged pastors and pastoral counselors are encouraging increasing numbers of their crisis-ridden parishioners to join self-help groups, particularly when recovery from an addiction seems to be crucial to solving other problems in living.

Since addictions of one kind or another often lie close to the heart of many people's proclivity to crisis, it is sound counsel to recommend sustained participation in a recovery group to parishioners suffering any particular addiction, and to lend pastoral support when recovering persons are ready to deal honestly with the harm they have caused others and to seek ways of making amends. Many pastors experienced in this kind of referral ministry can attest readily to how tempting it is to let self-help groups carry the largest burden of caregiving for some of their parishioners whose crises do have a basis in some kind of addiction. It came as a tremendous relief to Roger's pastor finally to conclude that most, if not all, of Roger's problems came down to a gambling sickness and that once he experienced success in a Gamblers Anonymous group, his other difficulties soon would abate.

It was not unreasonable for the pastor to fix upon Roger's gambling as the root of his pathology and to put his hopes in a recovery group as the key to cure. Roger's recent job loss clearly was a result of his gambling. His swindles of others were to cover gambling losses. He has lied to his pastor, spouse, and fellow Christians about the extent of his gambling. He was restless apart from "action," and obsessional about recovering his losses. He felt powerful whenever he was on a winning streak, and he deluded himself with elaborate narratives of how things would not only even out, but put him ahead in the long run. Roger was a true believer in his "system."

Roger's pastor is still working overtime to maintain the image of his parishioner as a committed Christian, striving to live as God wants him to live, who goes a little overboard here and there but only because of an impulsiveness that his gambling fever has pushed over the edge. If it weren't for (just) this (little) problem . . . Holding onto this naive picture of Roger as only a gambler out of control helped both pastor and congregation alike to look away from the more disturbing features of his character. Roger shows utter disregard for others' rights and well-being (for his wife, his investors, other women, and for his own pastor). His energy, enthusiasm, gregariousness, and penitence all mask a deceitfulness and manipulativeness. His service to the church has accomplished little more than covering over the irresponsibility of his life beyond the congregation, and it is fed by desire for self-aggrandizing power. As a leader, Roger is opinionated, contemptuous of others who have opinions with which he disagrees, and only *seems* to be a "good" man. In the church, he is servant to his own needs only, as he is in his relationship with Sue.

There are far more Rogers in the average Christian congregation than many pastors and laypersons like to acknowledge. Promising-looking on the outside, on the inside they are only partially socialized sociopaths. Their scams all too often are slathered with a thick paste of their long-suffering fellow Christians' patience, tolerance, hopefulness, and kindness. Roger's embarking on a process of overcoming his pathological gambling will be only a first step, though an important one, to his attaining God's likeness. If Joy's attainment must be by way of the constant, abiding presence of people who refuse to stop believing in her, Roger's must be by way of confrontation with a God who will not be mocked.

Convinced that Roger's foibles have resulted merely from sickness and not malevolence, his pastor and many in his congregation have opted for a compassion-based strategy that has driven Roger further into the illusion that he is subject to no limits whatever. Roger's faith, on the other hand, is formed by the symbols of a tradition that takes very seriously not only the grace and mercy of God, but also the terrors that inescapably befall those who persist in defying God's summons to righteousness. For Roger, those terrors will have to become the instruments of his salvation; God's forgiving face will be seen only after he has been willing to look into the terrifying face of his Maker and discover there the depth of his Maker's displeasure. God's "System" is one that Roger will not finally be able to avoid. When respect for this fact supercedes pity and anguish on the faces of Roger's fellow-Christians, and when their compassion flows from this kind of respect, healing can begin.

The pastors in these two cases are competent, caring professionals who minister out of a lively sense of calling. They consistently elicit grateful responses from their congregations and admiring words from their colleagues. Yet, each is overwhelmed by the recurrent crises in their parishioners' lives, by the conspicuous absence of learning from these crises, and by pain and dysfunctionality that seem destined to persist without surcease. They anguish over how to care more effectively. And they continue to search for a key to unlock the mystery of people's troubling inability to resolve difficulties not uncommon to the human condition and to live the abundant life God has promised all of us.

One "key" dangled before busy and concerned pastors is a list of professionals eager to provide intensive psychotherapy aimed at changing long-standing patterns of thinking, feeling, and acting. At the end of the process, it is promised, troubled parishioners will improve their relationships and general functioning sufficiently to reduce permanently the number and severity of crises in their lives. This key becomes especially attractive once it becomes clear that a parishioner's crises point to some underlying and problem-creating pattern of dealing with life as a whole. Then, competent pastors know they must accept their own limitations, for changing long-standing patterns is an arduous and protracted enterprise. When pastors are honest with themselves about the full range of responsibilities that claim their time and energy, and when they assess the training and experience necessary to work with parishioners whose problems have to do with the very structure of their psyches, they may be ready to admit that someone else might hold at least some of the keys to the kingdom, even a "secular" caregiver. The problem is that few severely impaired parishioners and their families can even begin to afford the therapeutic treatments now available without financial help. And those fortunate enough to have insurance coverage for mental health services quickly discover that what is not covered by the policies is usually what is most needed. Most important, however, for many of the most distressed parishioners, is to realize that not even long-term reconstructive therapy will bring about the transformation of soul that must be the pastoral counselor's primary concern.

*Esther's pastor, **Don,** left the hospital room with a sense of relief that for the first time in what had come to seem an eternity, his parishioner seemed finally to be feeling some hope. Four years ago, he saw Esther, then thirty-two,* *in his office for the first time, and worked out a referral to a psychotherapist for what he thought might involve at least a few months of therapy for depression and low self-esteem. He wondered if Esther's obesity might involve some kind of eating disorder, but trusted the therapist to get to the root of all of Esther's difficulties in any case. Two weeks following her first appointment with the therapist, Esther reported that the therapist told her that she had been molested as a young child, gave her a pamphlet to read, and recommended that she join an incest survivors group. Don supported Esther's decision to accept the therapist's suggestions.*

Almost a year passed, and Esther's distress seemed to be as intense as it was at the beginning. With Don's encouragement, she sought out a second therapist who told her that the feelings associated with memories of early abuse would go away by themselves and that Esther simply needed to learn to tell herself positive things throughout each day. As she and her pastor began to explore a third treatment alternative, Esther's husband was promoted in his company and transferred to another state. Don did not see the couple again until they returned to the community almost three years later. At that time, he saw that Esther was more overweight, depressed, and confused than ever. Esther found on her own a new primary care physician who recommended antidepressant medication. Just as she began feeling some positive effects from the medication, her colitis flared up, eventually requiring hospitalization. In the hospital setting, Esther appeared more relaxed and said to her pastor how wonderful it felt "just to lie here and let everybody take care of me."

Working with Esther's physician and a psychiatrist who began treating her, Don gradually learned more about his troubled parishioner. The oldest of seven children, Esther remembered her childhood as filled with perpetual conflict, needy siblings either beaten or ignored by both her parents, sexual abuse by a grandfather and an uncle, beatings by her mother, drunken family members and friends invading the household at all hours of the day and night, and never having enough food to eat or clothes for school. When Esther was fifteen, her mother died suddenly of a brain aneurysm. Repudiating her father's demand that she take over the household, Esther ran away from home, lived on the streets for several months in another city, met a drifter willing to settle down, married him, and gave birth to her first child at age sixteen. Her husband soon left her, and she has had no idea of his whereabouts from that time to the present. Esther stayed on welfare for over two years while she completed her GED, and then began working at various secretarial jobs. In his fourth year, Esther's son developed viral pneumonia and died. She now blames her inadequacies as a mother for the child's contracting the illness and for her failure to seek medical help soon enough. For the next four years, she sought solace in a series of brief, intense relationships, all ending with "screaming, hitting, crying, and blaming."

Feeling utterly out of control of her life, Esther began attending the single adults group of a large and vital Christian congregation. There, she met and fell in love with a man in the group who was studying for the ministry. He seemed to take great satisfaction listening to Esther and helping her with her problems. A year later, they married. Though he subsequently gave up his plans for entering the ministry, he has proved a successful salesman and loving husband, but now he is deeply troubled about his inability to please his wife. As his desire for Esther diminishes, Esther grows steadily more enraged and disappointed in her marriage, even as she confesses feelings of overwhelming guilt over not being a good wife. To this point, Esther has sought no contacts with any members of her family of origin. Her pastor oscillates between intense desire to help Esther and intense anger, and shares that he is having difficulty understanding and forgiving himself for getting angry with her.

Don has had to accept the unpleasant fact that for parishioners like Esther, referral sources may be both available and affordable without being competent. The first therapist, who came "highly recommended," imposed his inferences without the benefit of data that Esther would disclose only years later as a result of patient, supportive counseling from her pastor and a treatment team. She had to spend a year in a recovery group defending with all her might against the discoveries that were disguising themselves as depression and self-soothing overeating. A second therapist, implacably hostile to any and all notions of "repressed memories," simply dismissed preemptorily the entire framework with which her errant colleague on the other side of the debate had burdened her and, desiring fervently to rescue Esther from living her life as a "victim," insisted that she get on with it by means of a one-day-at-a-time approach. The only "keys" these therapists held out to Esther were to empty and windowless warehouses.

In spite of these outcomes, Don still looks for someone else whom he is sure must hold the power to heal Esther. In the present circumstances at least, he does seem to have reason to hope that Esther finally may be in competent hands. Her current therapists have at their disposal the resources to alleviate a number of Esther's distresses: colitis, eating problems, dysphoric mood, feeling emotionally cut off from her family of origin, the post-traumatic effects of early abuse, fears of dying from a brain hemorrhage, and chronic concerns over whether she and her husband will have enough money to live on. But can Don be sure that even these better trained and more experienced professionals will handle their inevitable anger toward Esther any better than he himself has? Might the heroics required fully to treat Esther be beyond them? Might they not for their own peace of mind focus their efforts only on Esther's raging symptoms because the chaos in Esther's soul will prove too much for them?

Don has struggled to keep up with his troubled parishioner's proliferating difficulties over a long period of time, and wonders if there ever will be an end to them. Collaborations with other helping professionals have been time-consuming, as have his own numerous visits with Esther. Now, he sees his irritation with Esther as a cause for self-blame. Like Sheila, Don is in bondage to the idea that angry reactions to parishioners are unworthy of a truly caring pastor and, as such, can have no positive value whatever. But Sheila began to extricate herself from her own captivity by using her feelings as an occasion for reflecting on herself. What could be especially helpful to Don is a willingness to let his feelings shed light on *Esther's* condition as well as his own. Were he to do so, he could realize that part of his anger is about failing to fulfill his unrealistic expectation that he provide soul-*cure* and not merely soul-*care*. Esther's thoughtlessness in not allowing herself to benefit from his ministrations has left her pastor floundering to preserve at least a remnant of his dream to be all things to everyone.

The anger in Esther that Don is unable to metabolize is in reality a sign of his parishioner's profound grasp of something fundamental in every human being: an insatiable yearning for communion, aroused in us by our Creator who has made us to live life together.

Esther's deep yearning was earlier scorned by those for whom she existed only as a sacrifice to their own cravings. And so, outrage after outrage and disappointment after disappointment have made of her a discouraged, discouraging, and despairing woman, whose rational powers, like Joy's, have become cunningly manipulative of attention and whose decisions are for sickness rather than health. But deep within herself, Esther knows that this is not how things should be, not how they are meant to be, not how *she* is meant to be. Her sighs that are too deep for words burst forth in rage—a rage that men and women who were created for fellowship with each other and God seem only to know how to discount, mistreat, corrupt, and eventually destroy one another. It is this rage that has reached deep into Esther's pastor to unlock his own long unacknowledged frustration that far too many of his parishioners live out their lives "sicklied o'er" with the pale cast of solitude when God is calling all of us to cherish each other as members of a community without boundaries on the earth or in time. When Don is able to accept that this is righteous anger, he may be able both to articulate and embody to Esther a vision of the kind of communion God intends between every human being. And Esther may begin to see that what she most longs for herself is something she can attain best by offering it to others.

What is perhaps most striking about all three pastors in the cases just reviewed is their apparent unwillingness to allow their parishioners *truly* to be in crisis, strange as it may seem to suggest so. As helpful as crisis intervention methodology has been to pastors and pastoral counselors in this generation, I continue to find surprising how little attention its exponents typically give to examining crisis experience from the perspective of faith. By contrast, the Bible frequently employs metaphors of crisis to describe how God impinges upon human experience, metaphors that can make a significant difference to all crisis intervention. Its central metaphor refers to the crisis-event of God's *judgment* on the world, in the light of which everything we have believed about our relationships within the created order and with God are suddenly called into question.

Near the time of Passover, several Gentiles came to Jerusalem to see Jesus. In the Fourth Gospel's presentation (John 12:20-36), their coming is a sign of God's intention to draw Jesus' public ministry to a close. Jesus then withdraws with his disciples to a place away from the crowds in preparation for what is yet to come, delivering himself into the hands of his enemies. The climactic verse of the passage, and perhaps of the Gospel itself, is at verse 31: "Now is the time of judgment (*krisis*) on this world; now the ruler of this world will be driven out" (NAB). Utterly startling to every first hearer of this vignette, beginning with Jesus' disciples and the fickle crowds who joined them, is his next words: the manner of Satan's defeat will be Jesus' own crucifixion, the humiliation and death of the very Word of God made flesh. For anyone considering even the possibility that the economy of our salvation could be so vested, all previously held priorities, commitments, values, strivings, and expectations will seem suddenly without foundation. In Jesus' day, the people asked, "How can you say that the Son of Man must be lifted up? Who is *this* Son of Man?" (John 12:34 NAB, emphasis mine). No doubt the disciples continued calculating more precisely their own places in the coming new order. But before all of them, an unfathomable abyss of uncertainty was opening, like a black hole threatening to envelop and hold them forever. In the face of the abyss, most of Jesus' followers joined forces with those who already were clinging to past certitudes for their very lives, and they crucified him.

This kind of crisis occurs in an event of genuine encounter with a God who "counters" all of the elaborate schemas we create in order to have a relationship with our Creator on our own terms ("for the law was given through Moses, but grace and truth came through Jesus Christ"—John 1:17 REB). Such an event annuls all our evasive maneuvers aimed at defining life in the ways most pleasing to us, irrespective of our Creator's purposes. In it sounds God's summoning Word annulling our own words that gush seductive descriptions of enhancements richly deserved and drown out the Scriptures' sobering reminders of what will be required of us if we are truly to live as God intends. When the truth of God reaches our inmost being, the deceits that have substituted for trust and obedience shatter, and with them, our own sense of security and groundedness. Our *reactions* to this divinely initiated crisis include a sense that judgment is being passed not only on specific things that we may have done or left undone, but on the whole of our lives. We and everything around us have become questionable. "The LORD God called to [Adam], 'Where are you?' " (Gen 3:9 REB). "Woe is me! I am doomed, for my own eyes have seen the King, the LORD of Hosts, I, a man of unclean lips, I, who dwell among a people of unclean lips" (Isa 6:5 REB).

But encounters with God that bring judgment upon us also bring grace and mercy. God's earth shakes in order to present an altogether new possibility to us, beyond our own devising: "peace." The peace of God that surpasses our own understanding is wholeness within ourselves and communion with our neighbors, with the entire created order, and with our Creator. It comes on the far side of crises of our own making and of the single, all-encompassing Crisis that hovers over human existence in the world as such, the judgment and promise of God. At first, God seems to hurl at us words threatening us with condemnation; this is the word of the "Law." But God's words can be heard also as an offer of forgiveness and reconciliation; this is the word of the "Gospel." *Both* forms of God's Word can traumatize us before we can recognize them as words of opportunity, for both call us to nothing less than drastic and all-encompassing changes that we will resist just as surely as we resist every challenge to the status quo falsely believed to serve our best interests.

Understood from the perspective of faith and theology, every crisis and crisis-reaction in life is *also* a sign pointing to the underlying condition of crisis in which all humanity dwells, standing at once under both the judgment and promise of God. Among the "opportunities" that all situational and developmental life-crises present, therefore, is the all-important opportunity to weigh every life-decision and lifestyle in the light of the life God calls us to live. It is uniquely given to pastors and pastoral counselors, as they help people deal with here-and-now, issue-specific crises, to invite their parishioners and clients to consider a new context for life as a whole, the paradigm for which is the suffering servanthood of Jesus of Nazareth. Servanthood also will be crisis-laden, but experience gained by facing the ordinary crises of life prepares us for its consequences. And from the vantage point of servanthood, ordinary crises themselves take on a new meaning entirely, as opportunities to hold fast in our trust of God, enduring faithfully to the end. For faith, the issue is not that of somehow attaining insulation from crises altogether, but rather of choosing the crises upon which we will expend the largest portion of our energies.

It is an interesting question why this orientation to crisis, amply expounded by some of the church's greatest theologians through the centuries, is so little emphasized in contemporary crisis intervention literature, even by writers ostensibly devoted to exploring the *pastoral* implications of that literature. One reason is crisis methodology's insistence upon the responsibility of counselees to work out their own courses of action for resolving a crisis. Caregivers are not to do anything that could be taken as imposing their own values. Laudable as it may be to encourage autonomous functioning and self-sufficiency, however, these are not ends in themselves, and though a strong ego may prove helpful to coping in some circumstances, it is not up to the challenge of sustaining a relationship with a Transcendent source of power, meaning, and value.

Another reason for ignoring theological reflection on crisis experience may have to do with the connotations aroused by the term "judgment" itself. Psychotherapists of virtually every persuasion with whom I have shared the theological orientation to crisis just described display shock, dismay, outrage, and contempt, in varying combinations, at the first hint that someone might "judge" someone else, even and especially when the judge might be God. "Judgment" suggests "guilt" and pathological systems built upon fostering even more intense feelings of guilt. And since carrying guilt is now alleged to be harmful to normal people and meaningless to the sociopathic among us, it would seem that we are best served by exorcising it from our psyches with all due haste. I am inclined to think that the intensity of reactions against the semantics of "judgment" suggests a residue of unresolved personal issues themselves warranting closer scrutiny.

Certainly, a spiritually nurtured and nurturing community of faith will have no stomach for a style of piety that coerces people into feeling only guilt about themselves and fear toward God. In God's own time, however, the gospel rightly proclaimed in and by that community will elicit in all of its hearers a sense of crisis that includes a perceived judgment on their lives and a summons to re-assess everything in the light of God's own purposive will. Pastors and pastoral counselors can help people deal with such an encounter when they themselves remain faithful to the Word that calls them to account also. Crisis reactions, then, encompass more than what Erich Lindemann once called normal reactions to threatening situations. There is a kind of crisis that is more deeply disturbing than he might have imagined: the crisis of being called to account by our Creator. Listening to this call, however, is the beginning of eternal life, now and forever.

(3) SUSTAINING THE GRIEVING

Of all the situational crises pastors and pastoral counselors confront, none is so relentless as people's experience of loss and bereavement. In *Necessary Losses,* Judith Viorst brought to our attention the sobering fact that we never fully finish with grieving; no sooner do we seem to be getting over losing one family member or friend than the ominous news arrives of still another's actual or imminent demise. Along with these losses, Viorst wrote, we suffer also from the inevitable separations that attend growing up and "moving on," as well as from the rupturing of relationships we had thought would endure any hardship. Also, there are still other kinds of loss with which sooner or later we will deal: cherished pets, hard-won jobs, physical and mental health, plans for the future, possessions, confidence in what we were taught about life, and perhaps even of faith and hope.

In every kind of loss, people expect and deserve a sustaining presence from their pastors that will comfort them in their sadness and strengthen them for the life ahead. Among the resources competent pastors bring to the task is training that includes the best insights into the grief process modern psychology has to offer. Psychologically viewed, grief reminds us forcefully of the pain to which we make ourselves vulnerable when we form attachments to things and people. Every such attachment requires of us a readiness to *de*-tach emotionally when the relationship is no longer possible or desirable, and to find other "love objects" while enduring grief sometimes so intense as to cripple us. The intensity of grief reactions makes plain how strong our attachment needs really are and how difficult it is to relinquish what satisfies them. But relinquish we do, and with the right kind of care from others the aloneness we feel does not immobilize us. Gradually, we withdraw our love for the lost object, re-establish the relationship in memory rather than in present experience, and re-invest ourselves in new relationships, especially when we receive from those who care about us their presence, support, understanding, encouragement, and even challenge.

As helpful as psychological studies are to working through grief, it is nevertheless unsettling to discover in them so little positive regard for the contribution faith can make to the grief-recovery process. For instance, many pastors have been told that inviting a grief-stricken parishioner to see his or her loss through the eyes of faith can get in the way of "normal" grieving by minimizing the reality and seriousness of the loss at hand. And even if it is the parishioner who introduces faith issues into the discussion, pastors are still warned not to dwell for long on them, lest he or she inadvertently reinforce avoidance and even denial of here and now tragedy. But we dare not set aside faith and theology so casually, for they broaden and deepen the context within which loss, grief, and the forging of new relationships must be dealt with. Three interlocking themes, all requiring the language of faith, are especially cogent to the understanding of life's necessary losses: the holiness of God, dying into God, and self-emptying (*kenosis*).

Liturgy and doctrine alike bring before us majestically the true "logic" of attachment: God alone is worthy of our unconditional love, and love for anything other than God finally runs the risk of collapse into idolatry. We trust in Christ and in the Spirit because, and only because, we experience them to be with God at and from the beginning; in the words of the *Agnus Dei* of the traditional eucharistic liturgy: "for thou only art holy; thou only art the Lord; thou only, O Christ, with the Holy Ghost, art most high in the glory of God the Father." We believe in the Scriptures and call them holy because we discover their words to partake of God's own holy, world-creating words and Word. The One who alone creates and is making all things new is our Alpha and Omega, first and last, beginning and end, and it is to this One that we owe our ultimate gratitude, loyalty, and service.

Part of the irony if not the tragedy of human existence in the world lies in the hard truth that an ultimate commitment to what alone *is* ultimate can be learned only through penultimate engagements with finite, conditioned creatures and causes that proffer our first foretaste of what constant, mutual, abiding love and commitment might be like. Alas, however, penultimate engagements, constellated in galaxies of contingency alone, fervently promise more than they can ever deliver. Luring us with false promises of a steadfastness not open to the things of this world, they can only mire us in fascination with the transitory and doom us to false hope, crushing disappointments, and frantic ploys to fill our emptiness with yet another fleeting attachment. Created for life in community, the transitoriness of all attachments can arouse in us such desperation for a lasting love that we unthinkingly throw ourselves at what in our more sober moments we know cannot last.

Our dilemma arises from the fact that all of our penultimate attachments—to our earliest caregivers and their symbolic representatives later on, as well as to abstract ideals and causes—retard our growth by binding us to an order of being that is always passing away even as they prepare us for a relationship with that One who is truly worthy of unconditional commitment. And yet, unconditional love of our all-surpassing, unconditioned Lover is possible only for those who learn the possibilities and the limitations of temporally-bound, contingent, and conditional attachments. Because this is so, the pain of learning to love God with all our being will be wrenching: we must learn to love all that God loves, while enduring constantly having what we have learned to love torn from us.

*It is past midnight, and the pastor opens the front door of the parsonage to admit **Oliver**, who called in considerable distress only minutes before. The pastor, having only recently arrived in the community, is meeting Oliver for the first time, and remembers that he had shaken hands with Oliver's wife, Ann, after last Sunday's worship service. It was Ann who insisted that Oliver come to the pastor's home.*

After apologizing for the lateness of the hour, and engaging in a few minutes of small talk, Oliver angrily told the pastor that he had "killed two patients today." He went on to elaborate that two heart patients on whom he operated in the early morning hours had failed to survive the surgeries. Oliver seemed filled with self-directed rage, cursing himself and exhibiting a state so distraught as to be beyond the pastor's ability to calm. Oliver repeated several times that he had the highest survival rate of all the surgeons on the hospital staff, that he had done everything possible both prior to and during surgery to ensure the success of both operations, and that the condition of both patients made surgery a last resort. Even so, he could not let go of his sense of failure that he had not saved them. He expressed to the pastor that he felt wholly responsible for all his patients, that he never gave up on any of them, that his patients placed their lives in his hands, and that when surgery did not prove successful, it was because he was not up to the challenge.

Later in the conversation, Oliver owned up to being partly intoxicated and that he had had a drinking problem for years. He related his drinking to a need to escape from his anxieties and made a promise that he would return to Alcoholics Anonymous on a meeting-per-day basis for the next few weeks. In follow-up visits with the pastor, Oliver shared a much longer history of alcohol and drug abuse than he admitted at first. He also told the pastor that for many years he had wondered whether God may be calling him to the ministry in order to "save souls." His new self-doubts about his ability to save his patients' physical health, the pastor reflected to himself, seemed to be feeding Oliver's sense that being called by God requires becoming a messiah. But in Oliver's case, becoming savior to others cannot alleviate his own sense of fragility for which no degree of competence and success can compensate and that no addiction can dull.

Oliver's world is crashing around him because the skills he has carefully cultivated and the people to whom he has devoted these skills no longer can assure him of the stable order of being for which he so longs, an order amenable to his prediction and control, in which his is the preeminent place. Having invested so much of himself in becoming a healer by mastering the tasks his profession assigns to its practitioners, Oliver has lost sight of the all-important fact that he is who and what he is by virtue of gifts not to be treated as possessions, and by virtue of a calling to glorify the One who has entrusted him with them. Neither those whom he heals nor his exquisitely honed skills will endure, but the God who embraces both is from everlasting to everlasting. As Oliver's idols tumble, he may be ready to face what truly is worth his utmost devotion, and to be healed from the sickness in his own soul.

From the perspective of faith, then, every human being is called to a love for the Creator that will require letting go of attachments to the very divinely created things of this world through which and for whom the expression of love is first learned and savored. Unless every grief situation can be appreciated as an opportunity to discern something of this truth, of what all losses are *for*, the "work" that every grieving person is called to do will be incomplete. Psychological perspectives on grief can bring us to the threshold of such a truth, but no farther, because psychology has no way of determining whether any possible object of our attachment is worthy of an ultimate commitment. Psychology cannot help us transcend our proclivities for idolatrous attachments; for this, we must keep faith closely at hand.

A second theme important for distinctively pastoral approaches to grief counseling is the indissoluble connection between abundant life in God and dying. In order to be in communion with God, as Jesus seems so fully to have been, all of our worldly attachments must constantly undergo change, and in every such change there is a form of death to confront, especially when detachment is in the direction of placing our whole selves in God's hands and at God's service. In Christ, God invites us into a relationship whose most profound symbol is a cross, the crucifixion of self-serving expectations, of hopes for a peace (*shalom*) given on the world's terms, of confidence in our powers of mastering things to our own satisfaction, of illusions about the permanence of earthly attachments and satisfactions, and of the self-deception that life is not meant to include suffering. For Jesus himself, the cross meant the relinquishing of Messianic expectations; for his followers it means renouncing the wish for a secure, assured existence that will make no demands.

In spite of the anguish that accompanies it, grief can help us see more fully our destiny in relation to the symbol of the cross, even as it can become the indispensable means for passing into that eternal life that is given only to those ready to traverse the path of sacrificial love. In this sense, grief is a kind of baptism, of dying with and into the Christ who represents vividly what new creation can be like for us on the far side of loss. There is a proper time for introducing considerations like these into grief counseling. But what expedites the introduction is not only a finely tuned sense of the right moment, which is a hallmark of all effective counseling, but also the discernment that dying, indispensable to the process of living, is an essential component of our spiritual maturation as well. Only as we are prepared to die the many deaths our worldly attachments make inevitable can we attain readiness for the fullest kind of living of all, with God.

*At forty-one, **Bill** has achieved more than many might hope for in several lifetimes. In his professional life, he is both naturally gifted and well-educated. He has traveled to many parts of the world to help major corporations solve difficult and delicate problems. When investment opportunities presented themselves, Bill made wise decisions that netted him considerable wealth. He has many friends, a happy marriage, a beautiful home, and children who seem to be following his example of energetic involvement in matters that are both personally fulfilling and worthwhile. He is a faithful husband and caring father, who has pursued a healthy lifestyle with due attention to diet and exercise. Bill has never smoked, and drinks only sparingly, primarily in social settings. He and his wife are active members in their church, where both volunteer more time than their pastor thinks they have available.*

For the past two months, Bill has had to confront the virtual certainty that his life will soon end. Cancer that was first discovered in his abdominal region has now appeared in the lungs and liver. Bill cannot fathom how he could have become a victim of such a disease. Bouts with anger are quickly followed by remorse, then bargaining, and finally with confusion and anger triggering the cycle all over again.

Bill's mother has no difficulty at all grasping the meaning of her son's terminal illness. A matriarchal figure in her strict, midwestern Church of Christ congregation, she attributes her husband's own early death (of cancer) to Bill's marrying a Jewish girl and, by virtue of that act of apostasy, separating himself from the protective environment of grace God has shed upon the community of his elect. Bill's failure to learn from God's first act of retribution, his mother seems to believe, is what is now bringing about his own death at the hand of this same righteous God. Bill's wife has been devastated having to deal with her mother-in-law while receiving no comfort from her own parents in her time of grief because many years ago they disowned her for marrying a Christian.

Bill's pastor is deeply worried about the "meaning" her suffering parishioner is now being forced to entertain in his deteriorating condition. Outrageous as the mother's theodicy is, the pastor muses, it is at least providing some alternative for Bill to a scenario of suffering and death for no good reason whatever, to which the universe will remain everlastingly neutral and unaffected. The pastor wonders how she can provide nurture if Bill chooses a pathway of placating a furious God. The steps to Bill's "reconciliation" with such a God she can only dimly imagine. Yet, it seems almost obscene to her to consider that cancer simply is one more of the many bad things that happen to people, and that this is all that can be said of Bill's life on earth in its final hours.

Bill's pastor has exercised good judgment desisting from offering her dying parishioner any focused pastoral interventions until she becomes less troubled by the seeming injustice of this good man's suffering and less awestruck by the shocking and egregious misrepresentations of God that are serving the cause of meaning for Bill's mother. Her effectiveness is seriously compromised by her captivation with false theological alternatives reminiscent of Calvin's defense of predestination as the more comfortable doctrine than its (only) alternative, fate. With more theological reflection, the pastor will begin to see clearly once again how faithless to the Christian gospel it is to seriously entertain the possibility that

Bill's dying is either a punishment from God or meaningless altogether, and that there are no other considerations possible. In the meantime, she can affirm Bill in whatever stage of the dying process she may find him and hope that her affirmation will help him better to accept his condition.

For Bill to reach the stage of acceptance, however, it will be necessary for him to reevaluate how strongly he wants to hold the Bible to its promise of "three score years and ten" and how firmly he wants to insist on his own deservingness in God's eyes. At this point in his confrontation with losing everything that has mattered to him, Bill is clinging not only to his accomplishments, reputation, and relationships; he is also grasping for a purchase on time itself, as if having more of it with which to enjoy his life could alone make that life worthwhile. It also may be that the theodicy that Bill's mother has perpetrated on her helpless victims has reached deeper into his soul than he has allowed himself to admit, and that for its dissolution Bill is demanding nothing less than the extension of life by divine dispensation.

When Bill and his pastor are ready to gather the colorful threads that bear witness to his life on this earth, and to begin weaving them into a tapestry that will enrich his memory in those who admire and love him, they and all who join in the festivity will find much to be thankful for, much to rejoice about, and much with which to sing God's praise. For Bill has indeed lived his life faithfully and to the fullest. He has poured his abundant energies into becoming successful honorably, giving himself lovingly to his wife and children, setting an example gladly for others to follow, and sharing in the ministry of God's people in the world. More time would allow Bill to do more of the same. But at the end of even re-alloted time, Bill still would have to face his greatest challenge of all, returning gratefully his life and everything in it that has made it what it is to the One who finally is its source and goal. His pastor may be able to guide him to see, accept, and finally to affirm that now is the time to face the challenge, that this is not a matter for lament, and that all of the sacrifices Bill has made on behalf of others have prepared him well for the hour fast approaching.

A third faith theme in grief counseling is self-emptying, the *kenosis* of Philippians 2:6-7. "His state was divine, yet he did not cling to his equality with God but emptied himself to assume the condition of a slave" (JB). Earlier in the chapter, Paul speaks to what the self-emptying life might consist of on the human plane: "Leave no room for selfish ambition and vanity, but humbly reckon others better than yourselves. Look to each other's interests and not merely to your own" (2:3-4 REB). How could such a theme be even remotely relevant to grief situations, in which people characteristically are too painfully dejected to acknowledge wider possibilities at all? The answer is: because psychological approaches to grief fixate on the notion that the love-objects we lose and those that will replace them have their meaning only as sources of our own satisfaction and love. By contrast, faith views love-objects not only as *sources* of love, but as *recipients* of love, as grieving persons become able to offer it. Along with encouraging grieving persons to form new attachments as help for their heartsickness, therefore, pastors and pastoral counselors also invite their parishioners/clients to involve themselves meaningfully in caring *for* others, knowing that it takes just such self-giving to tap into the real sources of energy for getting on with life. Further, such energy is itself finally *for the sake of* serving the needs of others; living faithfully includes striving to fulfill our own needs in order to better live for others. In the end, what we discover is that our needs are best satisfied precisely by counting our neighbors' needs more worthy than our own: we find our lives by losing them. Paul's christological hymn gathers observations such as these into a magnificent rhapsody on God's exaltation of Jesus: "Sharing the human lot, he humbled himself, and was obedient, even to the point of death, death on a cross! *Therefore* God raised him to the heights and bestowed on him the name above all names" (Phil 2:8-9 REB, emphasis mine).

*Placing her new year's calendar by the telephone in the kitchen, **Jane** writes a number at the top left corner, angrily reminding herself that it has been twelve years since the death of her spouse. Jack, once a robust, life-loving, highly successful salesman, Jane's "take-charge" lover, and their children's rock of strength and encouragement, suffered a major stroke at the age of* sixty. *Neither Jack nor Jane received, however, what Jane now calls the "blessing" of physical death. Rather, Jack has remained confined to a small bedroom, able to move from a bed to a chair only with considerable help, from herself and sometimes from others as well. He has become an ill-tempered purveyor of demands that Jane feels she is both obligated and unable to satisfy.*

Over the years, Jane has put on a cheery face at church. The coming of a young female pastor, **Deborah,** *afforded her an opportunity to acknowledge some of her usually well-disguised feelings. Deborah feels that she is taking the place of one of the couple's daughters, who has grown increasingly remote from her parents as the full extent of Jack's incapacitation became evident. Jack appears to have related to the new pastor in somewhat the same way, only in the role of a strong, good humored father who is both curious and solicitous about his "daughter's" well-being. Jane is using Deborah as a daughter with whom she can open up about a painful family matter. Jack's maneuver is to use her as the one with whom he can play hale and hearty. Deborah is experiencing discomfort and feelings of helplessness as she learns more about her parishioners' everyday interactions that they carefully keep hidden from public view.*

Jack's demands for only certain foods, served at room temperature "right on the dot;" his inability to estimate the time needed to get to the bathroom; his lack of interest in listening to Jane's news from the neighborhood; and his intolerance of her spending too much time away from the house on any single trip have drained Jane's enthusiasm for life. She tells her pastor of her loneliness and desperation, guilt-ridden that she prays so hard for Jack to die in order for her to be released from her obligations to him. "In sickness and in health," once a vow pledged out of love, has become a curse. In his own conversations with Deborah, Jack continues to exude forced humor and an overly robust acceptance of his condition, expressing gratitude that he and Jane have grown closer in their love during their "trial of faith." Deborah wonders to herself if Jane and Jack ever were truly close, and if Jane might have left Jack earlier in the marriage could she have seen what the stroke and his response to it would do to her life. She admires Jane's commitment to what she believes God is asking of her, but wishes Jane could find more inner satisfaction carrying out what she thinks God and the community expect of people her age. Then, Deborah reminds herself that she has not even begun to "connect" with Jack in a way that might help him

*open up to her genuinely and, by so doing, help her to grasp both his and
Jane's predicament more adequately.*

"In sickness and in health . . . ," but for how long? To Jane, long
enough to become a torment, abetted by a medical establishment
too skilled at preserving life for her own good. Bitter over the
reversal of roles that cruel forces of nature have thrust upon her,
Jane can see alleviation of her suffering only in terms of her
husband's death. Her limited and limiting vision has consigned her
destiny to the cardiac output and brain activity of a man who has
become little more than an object of loathing, and it is contaminating her spiritual resources with guilt in addition to self-pity. She
"knows she should have a better attitude," but perseveres in a
childlike judgment of her situation that it is all so unfair—to her.
The rock-solid foundation of her marriage on which she could rest
comfortably has been shattered, and with it the intimacy that Jane
equated with being taken care of. Ever a grateful daughter, with
hands outstretched to the man she thought would forever give her
all that her own father did not, Jane aquired very little experience
being a wife to Jack. She has nothing to draw upon for meeting the
kinds of adult commitments that spouses must meet if their marriage is genuinely to be a partnership.

In Jane, Jack found the perfect solution to his own inability to
be intimate as a co-equal. For him, loving a woman meant "keeping"
a woman, and Jane thoroughly relished the bliss of a marriage that
would legitimate being kept. Jack has encountered greater difficulties "keeping" his daughters; one left home at the end of high
school, married, and put three thousand miles between herself and
her parents, and the other daughter with great efficiency became
"too busy" to help much with her father's care. Unable to take care
of his women, Jack has lost their admiration and, unable simply to
share himself honestly, he now is bereft of anything in his relationships with them that could provide him satisfaction other than the
infliction of endless requests and tasks. Jack's perception that he
and Jane are having to endure a "trial of faith" is accurate. But he
fails to recognize that the jury is still out on whether the two have
a marriage at all.

Deborah is perilously close to losing her opportunity truly to minister to Jane and Jack. Her sympathy for Jane seems to know no bounds; she assures herself frequently that there is at least one person capable of affirming to Jane that she *does* know the troubles Jane has seen. It seems to her a foregone conclusion that Jane will have to struggle to the very end with Jack, short of help, and that it would be a blessing to all if Jane could get to the point of feeling better about her confinement. When she is with Jack, Deborah is caught in a swirl of resistance to being "daughtered," partially because she has experienced unwelcome memories about her relationship with her own father. But this resistance will serve the cause of obliviousness to Jack's wanting to find in her a surrogate wife who will allow him to feel powerful again. As the pastor increases in Jack's eyes, Jane can only decrease.

In an embrace deadly to her soul, Jane clings miserably to hated ideals of spousal "loyalty" and to the delusion that her relationship with Jack is and forever must be the center of her universe. To Jane, caring means fusing, and fusing means obliteration of connection with a larger human community for whom she is also and even more importantly called to care. Deborah is skilled at drawing to Jane resources that can help her get out of the house, get time for herself, get rest and relaxation, and in general get ready for the next week's imprisonment. What Deborah has yet to offer Jane is an opportunity to invest herself in worthwhile relationships with others besides Jack, and to help Jane understand how "natural" it is both to want such relationships and to seek them actively. Some of the new relationships likely will be of a "helping" variety, from which Jane can learn for the first time that self-emptying is not necessarily self-giving, and that self-giving can be a source of inner satisfaction rather than depletion and resentment.

(4) THE HEALING OF SHAME

For those willing to admit to keeping their faults and sins secret, there may be no feeling more painful than the anxiety that accompanies anticipation that their exposure may be imminent, that there will be no place to hide, and that in the collapse of concealment, there may be misery without end. Panicked, we rush for "cover" in order to seal off from public view what we are most sensitive about in ourselves. Rather than have our omissions and commissions, our urges, failings, offenses, vices, and vulnerabilities displayed, we hide them in ourselves, only to discover that the pain of staying in hiding is as intense as the pain of exposure, and that "hide-bound-ness" strips life of its connectedness and joy. But the discovery rarely leads to actions that might alleviate our fearful condition. Instead, our "hides" thicken, our wills stiffen, and at the first hint that our protective covering might be torn away from us, we arm ourselves for the fight of our lives. Losing our cover would leave us bereft of the semblance of personal integrity and honor we wish others to see and acclaim in us. After the loss of our public self, the only dwelling place remaining is the slough of shame.

Of all the distresses to which our souls are vulnerable, none is more contaminating of communion with God and fellowship with others than feelings of shame and their manifold manifestations in dysfunctional behaviors and relationships. Shame unleashes particularly devastating effects on our growth in faith. It is indeed a "shame" that this should be so, for there is no distress of soul to which the Christian faith speaks more eloquently than the feelings of unworthiness that shame generates. Every human being is created bearing the indestructible image of God, which is at once God's unfailingly compassionate and hopeful image of us. Of those whom God has so created, God is not ashamed. If "fear is driven out by perfect love" (1 John 4:18 JB), so is shame, in those who know God's image of them truly.

But if fear is a sign that we are still "imperfect in love," then shame is a cry of disbelief that God believes in us. Overcoming this disbelief is the way toward healing shame. In the following pages, I will elaborate on this claim in the context of discussing more fully the structure and dynamics of shame. Emphasizing positive as well as negative aspects of shame feelings, I will attempt to enrich the context in which shame is often understood. Throughout, I hope to make clear the power of faith in the healing of shame.

(a) "Who told thee that thou wast naked?"

> And they heard the voice of the LORD God walking in the garden in the cool of the day: and Adam and his wife hid themselves from the presence of the LORD God amongst the trees of the garden. (Gen 3:8 KJV)

Having eaten from the forbidden tree, the couple is overcome with dread at the prospect of facing their Creator. As young children cover their faces thinking that by so doing they can avoid facing discovery as wrongdoers, Adam and his "wife" have wrapped their bodies in coverings and they have taken cover in the trees to escape being seen for what they now fear they are. For both children and this couple, however, no hiding place suffices; exposure always threatens, punishment seems inevitable, and an anguished and inconsolable sense of failure and wretchedness begins its corrosive work on the soul. "For dust thou art, and unto dust thou shalt return" (Gen 3:19 KJV).

Already, I have made frequent use of words such as "cover," "hide," "discovery," "exposure," "face," "gaze," and some of their derivatives, because these are the words that suggest most vividly what shame most fundamentally is: a profound sense of unworthiness when things we want to hide about ourselves are exposed. Whether or not the things hidden are really "worth all the fuss," whenever we *believe* that their revelation would devastate us, our anticipation of their exposure generates fear. The exposure itself brings about the feelings to which the word "shame" properly refers, feelings that range from mild embarrassment (e.g., a fashion plate discovers that gravy spots on her blouse undermine her carefully cultivated spotless appearance), through humiliation (e.g., an athlete's string of victories are found to have been aided by illegal use of steroids), to utter mortification (e.g., a prominent jurist is arrested and convicted for harassing his former lover's daughter).

Part of the power of the Yahwist's story of "the Fall" derives from his deft use of a common symbol for being seen as we are with none of our carefully cultivated defenses intact: nakedness. When encourged to recall and to reflect upon their dreams, many people will share with a mixture of amusement and embarrassment a dream of being in a public setting without clothes. Usually, however, only the dreamer seems distressed about the situation, which suggests that a major function of nakedness dreams may be to remind us of how much we *fear* the exposure of what we feel most vulnerable about, of how painful even the anticipation of such exposure can be, of the lengths we are prepared to go to keep our inner selves protected from other people's unwanted gaze, and, ultimately, of the unrealistic quality of many of our fears. This last observation is one to which I will return shortly.

Typically, we react with at least some degree of shame for ourselves or for someone else when things like the following are exposed: weakness in facing a challenge; failures in competition; messiness, especially in connection with eating or elimination; physical defects, especially those associated with sexual attractiveness and potency; mental defects; losing control, especially of bodily functions and of feelings; sexual impulses, especially to watch, expose, pleasure oneself or fornicate with abandon; and aggressive impulses, especially to hurt or degrade someone. Deep down, most people feel that there is something "wrong" with them, if not involving one or more of the shameful characteristics just cited, then something else just as unpleasant to contemplate. When we are found out, we blush, cover our faces with our hands, and wish that somehow "the ground would open and swallow me up."

At whatever intensity, shame reactions almost always are overreactions that treat some one part of ourselves as if it is the whole, as if there is nothing else to us but the repugnant things to which we and others recoil in disappointment and disgust. Sometimes, what we hear from others reinforces the generalization we are ready to make about ourselves: "We are so disappointed in *you*." Such words may have been intended to express revulsion over something done or not done, but they are experienced as a condemnation of our whole being. Feeling contemptible to the core, we encounter great difficulty mobilizing our powers of self-reflection to determine the extent to which our negative self-judgment is and is not appropriate. We are unable to see what may be contemptible in us in relation to other aspects of ourselves that others do in fact respect. And so, "there is no health in us." Health in this situation will depend on using more effectively our God-given capacity to look objectively at things, including ourselves. When our self-reflection is guided by faith's understanding of who we are in God's sight, we will be able to face others' accusing and the debilitating self-blame to which we have subjected ourselves.

Susan, grieving over her recent divorce, found herself overwhelmed by a barrage of responsibilities she felt she alone was required to handle. Her job as a CPA demanded intense concentration and Susan felt she was losing this ability. Both of her two children were having unprecedented difficulties in school, for which her ex-husband blamed her. Her younger brother was dying of AIDS and was consumed by rage. Susan blamed herself for not providing her brother the kind of guidance her parents had conscripted her to give while they absented themselves from their own children's growing up. Now her aging and unhealthy mother and father were insisting that Susan become their primary caregiver, since, in their words, she no longer has duties to a husband.

Ardent in the practice of her religion, Susan only gradually allowed herself to share with her pastor her deepest hope that, somehow, she could make herself worthy of God's love by repairing the damage she already had done to her family. Becoming a more loving mother and daughter represented to Susan the only way of making up for her failures to this point in her life. Her greatest fear was that she would continue to bring havoc upon those she loved most deeply because of the disfavor in which she stood before God. At the height of Susan's anguish, she shared a dream. In it, she was attempting to drive an old car badly in need of repair up a winding road to an uncertain destination. It was winter, a high wind was blowing, and the road was icy. In the car were her children and all their possessions. Driving conditions worsened, and Susan ran the car into an embankment while trying to navigate a sharp curve. Slowly, she worked the car out, but it lost traction on the road, slid toward the edge on the opposite side, and plunged into inky blackness. Susan was shaking as she finished telling the dream.

The pastor was alarmed, and found herself disposed to attempt what for her would be an unconventional response to another's dream. Unclear whether the prompting in her was just a hunch, "gut instinct," or a word from the Lord, the pastor solicited Susan's permission to bring the session to a close by asking her to do something about which there would be no discussion until their next meeting. Though quizzical, Susan agreed. The

159

pastor asked her to retell the dream, but remain open to "working with it a little, right at the end." Reluctantly, Susan began the ordeal of reexperiencing her frightening dream.

When Susan reached the point of recounting her troubles getting the car out of the embankment, her pastor told her to throw the car into reverse, and with "pedal to metal" race the car over the edge on the opposite side. With a little encouragement, Susan did what was asked of her. With the car suspended in the air before commencing its fall into oblivion, Susan repeated what the pastor asked her to say: "well, well, I've gone and done it again!" Susan then burst out laughing, and then expressed surprise at her reaction. The pastor quietly concluded the conversation by confirming the time for their next meeting.

Several days later, Susan telephoned to tell about a peculiar experience she had had, which was quite unlike any other in her life. On the way to pick up two of her children at school, Susan felt herself wholly caught up by a warmth that she deemed love, a love that "had to be coming from God." The warmth of God's love overcame her sense of failing to live as God wanted, and from the time of the experience, Susan went on, she had felt nothing but relief and release. The pastor was especially interested in a particular detail in Susan's recounting of what appeared to be nothing less than a "conversion" experience. Susan said that as she basked in the sensation of warmth, she heard what sounded like singing, even the singing of her own church choir, but she was not sure what was being sung. The pastor asked her to hum the melody. It was "Are Ye Able." Unlike the brother of old, Susan had escaped the murderous plot of the Cain within her.

(b) For this, and every day, is the day of wrath

> I watched as the Lamb broke the sixth seal. There was a violent earthquake; the sun turned black as a funeral pall and the moon all red as blood; the stars in the sky fell to the earth, like figs blown off a tree in a gale; the sky vanished like a scroll being rolled up, and every mountain and island was dislodged from its place. The kings of the earth, the nobles and the commanders, the rich and the powerful, and all men, slave or free, hid themselves in caves and under mountain crags; and they called out to the mountains and the crags, "Fall on us, hide us from the One who sits on the throne

and from the wrath of the Lamb, for the great day of their wrath has come, and who can stand?" (Rev 6:12-17 REB).

Shame performs its destructive work on the soul primarily through our capacity for making premature and global negative judgments on ourselves and others. As I hope the previous section made clear, a lively and positively-hued faith can go a long way toward overcoming the consequences of such judgments. However, there is a more pernicious side to shame that is not so amenable to transformation by faith: *shaming* as an instrument of abuse.

Unfortunately, our capacity to feel shame makes us especially vulnerable to this kind of abuse, primarily because shaming is one of the most potent means available to us of ensuring others' compliance. Most people will go to great lengths to prevent someone's thinking and feeling badly toward them as persons. People who know this about human beings can use their knowledge to motivate compliance with appropriate rules and norms and help to bring about stability in their families and communities. They can also misuse their knowledge to gain and maintain control over others. The very young are especially susceptible to manipulation by being made to feel ashamed. Long before they are able to judge for themselves whether or not they are deserving of an elder's disappointment, disapproval, or condemnation, some already have been shamed mercilessly, by accusers bent on destroying their spirits. By verbal, emotional, physical, and even sexual abuse, human beings created in the divine image are shamed into submitting to others' demonic designs, only to feel at the end of their degradations gratitude that they are not any worse off.

Shame abuse cripples its victims both by making them mere objects of their abusers' satisfaction and by making them feel responsible for and deserving of their own unhappiness. Especially poignant today is the situation of those who bear the shame of incest. These are some of society's most emotionally scarred. Some become youth runaways, wandering the streets as drug abusers, prostitutes, and thieves. Others get through life with the help of dissociative disorders learned early as ways of denying intolerable assaults. Many incest victims strive to appear free of pain, but remain inwardly debilitated from vulnerability to shame feelings and the fears that everywhere accompany them.

Universally, persons entering adulthood with shame abuse carry with them the heavy burden of managing dependency, rage, and denial. It is a peculiarly perverse feature of our vulnerability to shame feelings that the more one *is* shamed, the more persistent can become the yearning for acceptance and approval, not only by others in general, but by the very shamer himself or herself. The most shamed among us typically bring into adulthood a yearning for others' positive regard that is so powerful that their behaviors become both influenced and even determined by others' reactions, real and anticipated. Some shame abused persons become "pleasers" who feel personally responsible for others' happiness. In their frantic desire to be caretakers, they can learn to appear attractive, mature, and competent, ready to give of themselves happily and without demur. The compulsive quality of their functioning, their *having* to be needed, is often covered over with astonishing efficiency, as is the fantasy underlying their behavior: "If I can and do meet others' even impossible demands, then I will be loved for myself." In their extreme dependency, they may seek out especially "needy" persons with whom to relate, persons whose own demandingness often manifests in the same kinds of abusive behaviors from which the shamed are desperate to be liberated. But instead of achieving the longed-for freedom by self-giving, the caretaker finds herself/himself caught in an escalation of the cycle of shame without knowing why.

Along with strong dependencies, shamed persons carry heavy burdens of anger over having been shamed so often and so intensely. To this anger is added the resentment of caretaking itself, for in making other people happy, caretakers' own needs typically go unmet and their frustrations compound. Anger and resentment coalesce only in imperfectly suppressed rage, the management of which steadily depletes life energy. Early in life, the shame-filled learn not to deal openly with their feelings, for to do so would put them at risk. But then they must work diligently to keep the dangerous feelings disguised even as the disguise itself becomes another source for feeling ashamed. Are not Christians to love their enemies and do good to those who persecute them? The hint of a feeling to the contrary, even toward someone who is not only an enemy but a destroyer, can evoke still more feelings of unworthiness, fended off by still more frantic caretaking. It is little wonder that for some, denial of feelings altogether might seem the safest course.

In Jeremiah 31:29, the prophet is quoted as saying "The fathers have eaten a sour grape, and the children's teeth are set on edge" (KJV). What we are learning in this present era about the consequences of abuse for future generations could not be a more vivid exemplification of the prescience of this dramatic utterance. With the discovery that most shamers and abusers are themselves shamed and abused persons, the sobering implication has begun to dawn for many of us that, if unchecked, exploitation of the human capacity to feel shame will persist across many generations. Those caught in the cycle of abuse struggle valiantly not to appear shamed, shameful, or ashamed either in others' eyes or in their own. Disguises vary. For instance, some express their feelings of unworthiness and rage by submissively taking care of others who will continue to abuse them; others block awareness of their condition with the help of the myriad substances all too readily available for the unwary, or inflict abuse on others in proportions even exceeding the abuses they have suffered from others. To all such entrapped persons, Jeremiah's vision of a new order in which "every one shall die for his own iniquity" (v. 30) must seem utterly incomprehensible, if not ludicrous.

Everything that once may have been "godly" seemed to have gone out of **Dan**'s *life, as if before the very eyes of the older members of the congregation who remembered Dan as a perfect little boy growing up. For months, Dan had been belligerent to a number of his Sunday school class members whenever they expressed concern for him and for his wife,* **Phyllis,** *and he had rejected out of hand several concrete offers of help after being fired from yet another job. Dan felt that he deserved better opportunities than those so far presented, which were beneath him.*

The pastor knew that Dan's recent firing had been the result of hitting his supervisor hard enough to send him to the hospital, and that Dan was facing, at the least, a civil suit, and possibly arrest on a charge of assault and battery. Phyllis, too, was a victim of Dan's temper, although his violence at home seemed under control since his pastor had helped him reach a no violence commitment to her. Dan expressed pride in himself for being big enough not to let Phyllis bother him as much as she used to. He was unwilling to make a no violence pledge with respect to anyone else, citing the possibility of having to confront people who threatened to harm his family and his mistrust of the help the police might give in such situations. It was difficult for the pastor to put out of his mind the night he himself felt threatened by the fury he saw in Dan's eyes. He wished he had been around to see something of the perfect little boy Dan perhaps once might have been.

As the pastor learned more about Dan and his growing up, he began to wonder if things really had been better once upon a time. Dan's school history was one fraught with academic difficulties, misbehavior, truancy, and even suspension. Neighbors recalled that Dan blew off his parents' concern over his violations and that he characteristically complained that his father was always on his case. From his first part-time job at fourteen to a well-paying, secure position at his present age of thirty-one, Dan's employment history was a repetitious sequence of leaps from one job to the next, sometimes by his own choice and more times because of terminations. He seemed to have no difficulty selling himself to other prospective employers in spite of his job history, and often was described as a "charmer." But to his parents, Dan constantly complained that he never seemed to find a job worthy of his talents, that he was always misunderstood and mistreated by his employers, and that people in the business world could never be trusted. On two occasions, Dan hired a lawyer to sue his employers, without success in either case. Dan kept the details of his family's finances hidden from Phyllis out of the conviction that she could not manage such things as well as he, yet he was persistently hounded by creditors whose bills he had not paid. A number of loans from both his own parents and Phyllis's were long overdue. Phyllis's father wrote them off in his mind and vowed never to offer money to Dan again, while Dan's parents nagged him constantly with their need for the money, even while lending him more. Dan was surprised at the intensity of his creditors' concerns, and blamed them for not appreciating all he was trying to accomplish in life.

Clearly, his pastor mused, the choices Dan made about how to live his life were anything but productive. Dan acted selfishly and gave no thought to the effects of his actions on others. He was abusive to those who loved him and who cared about his welfare, and he seemed utterly incapable of giving anything of himself to those who labored on his behalf. The pastor did not find comfort in Dan's parents' grateful reminders that at least their son wasn't on drugs and didn't carry on outside of his marriage. "How can I help someone I dislike as much as I dislike this man?" the pastor asked himself.

It is not difficult to sympathize with Dan's pastor. He is aware of his mounting dislike for his parishioner, who seems bent on resisting not only his own best efforts but the help with which others are surrounding him as well. The pastor is especially reactive to reports that Dan has physically abused Phyllis. Acknowledging his feelings, however, does not release the energy the pastor knows he needs in order to see Dan through the crisis of the moment. He knows how to structure a series of problem-solving interventions that could get Dan's life organized around more constructive behavior patterns, but he lacks the will to begin.

For all his troubles, Dan has continued to spew out an astonishingly exaggerated sense of self-importance and arrogance. He believes himself to be a special person who deserves wide-eyed appreciation and exceptional treatment from others. From at least his early adolescent years, Dan has constantly taken advantage of other people for his own purposes and to the present moment seems wholly unable to understand and accept that anyone could be angry with him. He makes a great display of interest in others' concerns and of a desire for mutually supportive relationships. Dan's publicly caring stance, however, is pretense only, self-serving to the core. He harbors wholly unrealistic notions of what he can accomplish in life, regards others as only serving his own ends, and blames even those closest to him when things do not go the way he thinks they should. From his early school years, Dan's ability to charm people who otherwise should be irritated and even disgusted with him has helped him to cover over a multitude of offenses. *When* might Dan have been easier to like?

In his case, there is no when, unless we can bring more clearly into view *other* things covered over by Dan's everybody-loves-awinner kind of charm. Dan's braggadocio and defiant style seals off from others, as well as from himself, the terror of being found with weaknesses or defects. The sense of mortification (literally, shame unto death) attending unwanted exposure is something from which Dan protects himself literally at all costs. Criticisms, alluded to as "hassles," threaten Dan's soul constantly with meltdown. That Dan was remembered by church members as a perfect child is food for thought. One thing such memories show is that Dan learned early how to present himself winsomely whenever it was in his best interest to do so. Church members disposed to believe the best about people would have been given many impressions on which to draw their conclusions about Dan. More important though, these same church members also made it possible for Dan, at least when in their company, to be the kind of person they, in fact, wanted him to be. To young Dan, influenced strongly by his parents' active involvement in the congregation, the church members he knew were the kind of important people in whose company he himself could feel important. Their "mirroring" allowed him to see in himself qualities worthy of respect because they actually were respected, and possibilities worth developing because they elicited others' admiration. He had a sense of belonging because those who mattered to him opened a place for him in their hearts and lives.

Why such mirroring proved insufficient is the most important question for Dan's pastor to answer as he struggles to overcome unpleasant feelings about his wayward parishioner. A satisfactory answer can help the pastor regain enough empathy with Dan to restore the threatened pastoral relationship. Perhaps Dan's self-image already was shaky by the time he began to experience warmth, nurturance, and positive regard from others outside his own family. Perhaps Dan did not experience enough interaction with church members over a long enough time to overcome the negative mirroring that pummeled him during his school years. Perhaps those who loved Dan the most still proved inadequate to the task of helping him identify and deal with his deepest feelings of vulnerability at their most intense. Perhaps all of the above and then some. Whatever the contributors may have been to the style that has become so discomforting to others, the fact is that for Dan to transcend his false grandiosity, he must confront his equally false perception of emptiness within, armed with the truth that radiates from the faces of patient, empathic, friends.

Long-term reconstructive therapy in individual and group settings promises Dan a way toward more easily tolerating his mistakes and failures; taking realistic pride in his own accomplishments without depending on others' adulation for his sense of self-worth; reciprocating others' care out of a desire for their own enhancement; self-giving even to those from whom he is not likely to receive anything in return; and allowing relationships to matter enough to grieve their loss. The success of such therapy will depend heavily upon the therapist's making himself or herself empathically available during the times of intense sadness, and even depression, which inevitably will accompany Dan's journey into the heart of his vulnerabilities. As attractive as the alternative may be of long-term therapy for Dan, however, his pastor knows that it is not a realistic option. Dan's family members do not have the resources necessary to cover the cost themselves. Further, in the light of available studies on the effectiveness of reconstructive therapies in general, even if the financial resources were available to provide Dan such treatment, it is debatable whether they should be so invested. Short-term professional interventions will be possible from time to time, of course, but primarily for symptomatic relief. And so, daunting as the prospect may initially appear, if Dan is to be healed at all, he will have to be healed in the company of his Christian friends who see him as he *really* is: cherished by the One whose image he bears and whose likeness is the proper end of all our striving.

Dan's feelings of emptiness, and their denial, are what set him most at enmity with himself, others, and his Creator, and provoke his most outrageous acts of self-aggrandizement. Both the feelings themselves and their denial must become the focus of a very aggressive caregiving that seeks to excise the malignant notions upon which they are based. To the more clinically-minded, these notions may be more like perceptions of a pathologically formed no-self. To theological dualists, they are the deceptions of the Devil himself. However they are viewed, their effects include a terribly distorted spiritual vision on the basis of which Dan continues to draw both erroneous and blasphemous conclusions about himself. What he most needs are lenses of faith through which he can see clearly the benign, affirming gaze of his Creator, whose love for him, experienced first in the love of those who also know God's love, can free him from the desperation of having to command admiration from others in order to feel alive.

Dan's false notions about himself are also conveyed by sadistic voices from the abyss of his soul that taunt him unceasingly with lies about his inadequacies, incompetence, unworthiness, and un-lovableness. His narcissistic defenses may be capable of shutting them out most of the time. But these voices will not be overcome finally except by those willing and able to shout them down, to drown their cacophony with the resounding chords of truth: we are made, and wondrously made, in the very image of God, for part-nership. In calling us to account, God always and everywhere offers reconciliation and not condemnation. We have neither reason nor right to judge ourselves more harshly than our loving Creator judges us. We do not have to be masters in our own house, and we do not have to gain mastery over others in order to be someone. He who *is* our master desires not to master us, but to be with us and to share God's own eternal life. ("No longer do I call you servants, for the servant does not know what his master is doing; but I have called you friends, for all that I have heard from my Father I have made known to you" [John 15:15 RSV].)

As unlikable as Dan has made himself in the eyes of practically everybody who knows him, he has not yet extinguished all the signs of who he really is in God's sight. And though his pastor had been feeling that looking for something good in Dan was like sifting through rubble left by a series of explosions, he nevertheless found himself struck by two remarkable facts. First, the learning disabili-ties that had to have made a purgatory of Dan's school years did not prevent him from gaining enough knowledge and skills to ensure more than moderate successes in the workforce. Second, for all of Dan's fears of failure, he has continued to risk rejection by competing for better and better jobs. His pastor notes that many of Dan's friends believe him to be destined for even greater success in spite of the fact that his oppositional behavior seems to have brought him to the brink of ruin. In seeing more in Dan than the evidence suggests may be there, these friends may have grasped better than the pastor that what *is* there, in Dan and in all of us, always is more than we are apt to reckon. Perhaps both pastor and congregation together can provide Dan sufficiently consistent imaging of himself as God images him to free him *from* his unnecessary and dysfunctional self-defenses and to free him to discover for the first time what his God-given gifts of freedom and reason are *for*: service to all whom God loves, in whose service we truly find ourselves. The process of effective caring is already beginning in Dan's case. His pastor now can see in his recalcitrant parishioner at least something of the capacity to attain to the likeness of his Creator, even though that capacity seems dangerously atrophied in the present circumstances. What the pastor continues to see in Dan can make all the difference.

(c) "I blush to lift my face to you"

> At the evening sacrifice I came out of my stupor and falling on my knees, with my garment and cloak torn, I stretched out my hands to Yahweh my God, and said: "My God, I am ashamed, I blush to lift my face to you, my God. For our crimes have increased, until they are higher than our heads, and our sin has piled up to heaven. . . . Yahweh, God of Israel, by your justice we survive as the remnant we are today; here we are before you with our sin. And because of it, no one can survive in your presence" (Ezra 9:5-6, 15 JB).

For all too many in our society, the burden of carrying shame feelings is crippling to the soul. So devastating are the consequences of both the negative and the destructive manifestations of shame that we might indeed wonder whether anyone can be truly healed of them. Perhaps this is why so many therapeutic approaches to healing the shame-sick attack not only the shame feelings themselves, but as well the *capacity* to feel shame at all, as if vulnerability to shame is something like an immune deficiency all of us are better off without. In contrast with such approaches, I think that the manifestations of shame, painful as they are when experienced, are properly understood not simply as destructive, but as derangements of a capacity that is part of that very goodness that constitutes our God-given humanness.

The capacity to feel shame assists us to regulate our participation in communities of persons whose images and expectations of us are important for our growth. Because we need meaningful connections with others at every stage of our lives, it is important that we can be affected by those others' perceptions of and reactions to us, even when we decide to act in ways that disappoint them. Knowing that we matter to others, and having available to us their hopes, expectations, and even demands, equips us with a large fund of possible ways of functioning from which to compose a sense of self or personal identity. More often than not, we accommodate to the wishes of those upon whom we are most dependent and those who matter most to us, because we need and desire their continuing support and approval. Fearing the loss of such support, we remain vigilant for any signs of shifting reactions to us, and usually we make whatever adjustments in our behavior, attitude, and bearing we perceive to be called for. Early in life, we do most of the adjusting. Later, we discover that others in our lives are engaged in similar kinds of monitoring, because our reactions to them are important to their own sense of well-being. For everyone, the capacity to feel shame when we have disappointed someone, when we have failed to keep ourselves in line with others' expectations, when another turns disapprovingly away from us, when we have been caught in something unacceptable, or when others express concern over the direction our behavior might be going serves the interests of our social nature well. Shame is a necessary inhibitor of the interest, excitement, and enjoyment leading to behaviors that could alienate us from those we most want and need in our lives. In those for whom other people's reactions still are important, inhibiting certain affects by means of activating the capacity to feel shame can extinguish the behaviors associated with the affects, swiftly and totally. For example, though shaming can be overdone by parents, it is generally a more effective punishment for misbehavior in children than is spanking; physical pain is soon forgotten, but the threat of ostracism is felt long after the particular conflict is resolved. Precisely because shaming *is* so effective as a regulator of behavior, its uses must be carefully thought out and continuously reevaluated.

Those who tend to react angrily to the suggestion that shame plays a positive role in human life seem also to operate out of a generally disparaging view of social conventions as evils to be overthrown in the name of individual freedom and authenticity. *If* the individual as such is of overarching significance in all societies, then it might follow with some justification that no human being ever would have the right to shame another in the interest of bringing about conformity to the expectations of a particular social group. But the eventual outcome of such an anarchist view would be a shame-less generation of dis-connected individuals each doing her and his own thing. That this description comes close to our own society's current aspirations is mildly unsettling, to say the least. More hopeful is the fact that many now feel acute embarrassment over the competitive, acquisitive, consumptive, addictive, and destructive excesses of our current lifestyle, obscenely celebrated as the just desserts of the most powerful nation on earth. Our future lies more with those who still can feel as Ezra did: "My God, I am ashamed, I blush to lift my face to you, my God."

(d) "God saw all that he had made, and it was very good"

Once we experience even a glimpse of the awesomeness of being human, and with gratitude seek to fulfill our unique and glorious calling on earth, even the possibility that any of our kind ever could be burdened with feelings of shame and unworthiness has to appear, at best, paradoxical, and at worst simply shocking. For have we not been told that we, so vulnerable to shame, are creatures who have been made in the very image of God? Have we not been told that we, capable of feeling ourselves to be the most contemptible and despicable of all God's creatures, are created little lower than the angels? Sinners though we are, are we not *forgiven* sinners, part of a redeemed order that nothing on earth, even our own misdoings, can separate from the love of God in Jesus Christ? How is it, then, that with the transformation of our guilt made possible in God's redeeming and sanctifying love, shame is still able to destroy mercilessly every remnant of self-esteem, self-confidence, and hope to which God's beloved may still desperately cling?

However we may choose to deal with these anguish-inspired questions, the one thing we will not be able to do convincingly is to minimize the existence of shame in such a way that its healing can be taken for granted. As has been discussed in the previous sections, the negative side of our capacity to feel shame is a very powerful disposition to translate another's disapproval of something about us into a judgment about ourselves as a whole. And the pernicious side of our vulnerability to shame lies in our not easily extinguished susceptibility to abuse, by others and by ourselves. If we are to be healed from the diabolical excesses of shame (diabolical precisely in the sense that these excesses divide us inwardly and cut us off from a right sense of our true nature), we will have to acknowledge what we may most resist acknowledging, that there is a divine purpose to our being created shame vulnerable, even though we seem almost predestined to endure shame experiences all out of proportion to any conceivable good that might come from surviving them.

At the risk of being misunderstood as blaming the victim, especially a victim of abuse, I think it important for even those who carry the full burden of such travesties to wrestle with the possibility that their feelings of shame are in fact appropriate to their actual condition and that it is good that they can feel shame if such a feeling is warranted. Only by struggling with such an offensive notion can we discover that many times we do *not* in fact deserve to feel the way we feel. But in spite of the ever-present and incalculably variegated possibilities for shame to work destructively on our souls, the capacity to feel shame and to reflect on what actual feelings of shame may mean for us in particular situations are crucial for human life in community. Vulnerability to shame, for all the pain it inflicts, is an indispensable sensitivity that protects us from the catastrophic consequences of being ostracized by those whom we most love and need.

For the healing of unwarranted shame, what is required is a process that will transform the devastating consequences of its excesses without inhibiting our capacity to feel shame in the first place. A good place in which to see such a healing process at work is in programs of recovery from the various kinds of abuse for which "Twelve-Step" programs have been developed. Whether for alcoholics, drug addicts, overeaters, overspenders, sex addicts, compulsive gamblers, or abusers, these programs share many insights in common and approach the recovery process in many of the same ways. In them is to be found a great deal of wisdom for overcoming hypersensitivity to others' reactions, dispositions toward self-blame and self-abuse, and patterns of inflicting shame and abuse on others in order to ease one's own woundedness.

Of particular importance in all recovery programs is the emphasis placed on coming to terms with the reality of one's condition in a supportive group of caring people who have "been there." Those committed to the recovery process know that their fellow sufferers and persecutors will continue to delude themselves from time to time, even during the recovery process itself, and so they are prepared to be strongly confrontive, but out of the conviction that lasting change is possible even in those whom others see as beyond all hope. Their patient acceptance and affirmation, especially of those hardest to accept and affirm, infuses the unloving and the unlovely, often for the first time in their lives, with the spiritual power necessary for confronting and transforming the hard truths about themselves. Those who have "hit bottom" now can face the truth because the truth comes to them relentlessly but in love, not a swarmy love made vapid by sentimentality but a love that actively and genuinely seeks their own best interest and that of all those their lives touch. It is a love demanding change—there will be no support for the continuance of destructive patterns of behavior, whether of oneself or of others—but it is a love that is constantly building up (and building back) those struggling to make the change.

Mired in shame that aberrant behaviors, addictions, and dysfunctional relationships all fail to cover over, persons willing to risk giving themselves to the ministry of others in recovery soon find that those who best know their inmost deficits, needs, and lusts also look upon them with faces filled not with selfish designs, seduction, and disapproval, but rather with compassion. Grace and peace break in where previously there lurked fear, crippling dependency, and rage. Truth begins its redeeming work of overcoming denial and self-deceit. Feelings of worthlessness, the callouses of degradation, are left behind in the human spirit's ascent toward that primordial, brooding Spirit who even now is triumphing over dissolution, destructiveness, and purposelessness.

Shame-filled shamers afflict their victims most noticeably with contemptuous words, straying hands, pounding fists, or a thrusting phallis, demonically transmitting the excesses of previous generations that reduce life to an emptiness howled in rage. Nightmarish as the memories are of such horrendous violations of personhood bearing God's image, call, and hopes, even these memories cannot fully portray the ultimate transgression against the human spirit to which shame cries its piteous and ineffective protests. That transgression is conveyed on the face and in the countenance of the offender, in the "looks that kill," of disappointment and disgust that annuls the very right of the other to be in the presence of the ones she or he has displeased. We may be tempted to flee these looks at all costs, even while bearing egregious assaults as somehow fit punishment for imagined offenses against our accusers.

But more powerful than these devastating looks is the power of empathic listening; of words carefully kept to a minimum; of voices choked with pain but sounding out hope; of penetrating eyes that look both into and beyond the shambles of a wounded spirit to see and to reflect God's promise of abundant life here as well as in the hereafter; and of mouths drawing upward into smiles, if not in delight at least in encouragement. The healing of shame begins when the ashamed notice in others' faces a countenance of respect, understanding, compassion, and hope; when they hear in others' voices softness, kindness, assurance, affection, and delight; and when they learn that these are the faces and voices of people who are with them and for them, especially when dis-eases threaten newly-won integrity, on the side of the abundant life that God intends and empowers us to live together.

Dorothy sat limply in the chair her pastor offered her, staring impassively at the floor, her face bowed in shame. Her skirt was wet from her rapidly *perspiring hands. With a tense voice, she slowly managed to tell her pastor that she and her husband, **Bill,** had spent the previous night at the adolescent psychiatric unit of the community hospital, where, with their family physician's help, they had taken their teenaged daughter for treatment. The daughter had become depressed to the point of openly talking about suicide. Two hours ago, Bill left the house angrily after throwing his breakfast plate against a wall, hurling epithets at Dorothy for failing to raise the girl properly, and blaming the biological father for poor genes.*

Dorothy accepted the full blame for her daughter's condition. With tears pouring down her face, she cried out that her daughter was being punished for Dorothy's "sickness and corruption." Dorothy then began a litany of bitter self-denunciations that spanned a major portion of her forty years on earth. She blamed herself for seducing her father to have sex with her when she was seven; she blamed herself for not preventing her mother's escalating problems with alcohol abuse, and for all the problems between her parents; she blamed herself for multiple sexual encounters in her college years, often with married men; she blamed herself for her first husband's business failures and subsequent suicide; she blamed herself for breaking up her present husband's first marriage; she blamed herself for being an unworthy parent to his two sons; and she blamed herself for spending too little time with her seriously ill grandfather.

In the two years he had known Dorothy, the pastor had found her to be an eager and conscientious church worker, faithfully present in worship every Sunday, and though somewhat shy, she was courteous and generous in her expressions of appreciation for his sermons. His two visits to Dorothy's home had given him opportunity to meet her husband, but not any of the children. To all outward appearances, Bill seemed a gracious host. But the pastor had been wondering why he never came to church and had promised himself that he would bring up the subject on his next pastoral call. He felt utterly unprepared for the Dorothy who now sat before him, desperate in her pain and all but unreachable in her self-loathing. His kaleidoscopic reactions to the material Dorothy spewed forth intruded upon his concentration and left him confused and anxious about when and how to respond effectively.

At the moment of his greatest distress in the conversation, the pastor happened to catch a glimpse of his own partly obscured reflection in a windowpane just behind Dorothy's head. The look on his face surprised him.

It was not the look of the confused, overwhelmed listener he was experiencing himself to be. It was a look of understanding, caring, compassion, and acceptance, just the kinds of responses he sought to convey to all troubled parishioners in their times of deepest distress. Though he knew he was straying from attending to Dorothy's words and feelings, the pastor allowed himself to drink in what was expressed in his own eyes on the windowpane. He focused intently on what he had seen and allowed himself to trust the image as genuinely representing his deepest reactions to Dorothy. As Dorothy approached the end of her self-denunciation, the pastor gently commented to her that she did not look at him as she told her story, and that he wondered what her reaction might be to what she saw on his face. Puzzled, Dorothy looked up. The pastor asked her what she was seeing. Dorothy replied: "kindness, pain." Then, he asked: "What would it be like for you to see yourself that way?"

In the few minutes remaining of this first of several meetings, Dorothy expressed amazement that her pastor could look upon her so positively after hearing all that she had told him about herself. She remembered the blessing that concluded all the meetings of the youth fellowship during her adolescent years in the church: "and the Lord make his face to shine upon you and give you peace." The pastor suggested that this might be something to say to herself in the days ahead as she committed herself to deal with everything about her that she felt made her unworthy. After the worship service the following Sunday, Dorothy greeted the pastor with a jubilance he had not seen before, while her husband, Bill, accepted the greetings of several members of the congregation.

Shame is put to rout finally in the presence of the One who always believes in us more fully than we believe in ourselves, in whose presence there is mercy from everlasting to everlasting. The pastoral counselor's distinctive role in the healing of shame can be none other than to offer as many times as necessary, until the soul can sing its truth with joy unspeakable, the divine blessing that turned Dorothy's heart to God:

May the LORD bless you and guard you; may the LORD make his face shine on you and be gracious to you; may the LORD look kindly on you and give you peace.

NOTES

PART I

1. To many of the ancient Greek philosophers, *arche* meant "essential form" or "standard," which holds us in being as what we are. The eternality of form provided the basis for the philosophical criticism from Zenophanes forward of the Greek Olympian religion, by appealing to something other than the gods as ultimate; unlike the forms, the gods and goddesses have not always existed. More important, however, the Greek philosophers understood that the eternality of form ensured the presence of form in the here and now.

2. The LXX Genesis 1:26 speaks of humanity "in our image, after our likeness" (*en eikoni hemon, kath' homoiosin hemon*), while 1:27 and 9:6 both refer to our being only in the image (*eikon*) of God. Given the importance of the terminology for users of the Greek language, it will be a matter for later reflection that after Genesis 1:26, *homoiosis* (likeness) is rare in the LXX Old Testament and occurs in the Greek New Testament only at James 3:9. As if to position himself firmly in the tradition of Hebrew thinking, the first-century Jewish philosopher, Philo, minimized the importance of distinguishing between the two words, and interpreted the *homoiosin* of Genesis 1:26 as simply an amplification of *eikon*, in the sense of the faithfulness of the image to what it represents. In Philo's view, having affirmed this relationship once, the Jewish scriptures did not need to do it again.

3. In one of the most heroic efforts in modern times to restate these alternatives convincingly, Karl Barth (CD III, 1, pp. 349-50) proposed that we regard the negativities of finitude as merely a "shadowside" (*Schattenseite*) of creation, distinguishable from those regions of finite existence whose origins are in active resistance and opposition to God's dominion (*Das Nichtige*). Barth recognized that there is more to be endured in the created order than the chaos that human sinning injects; there *is* something that is not as we would like it to be about things generally, that is not to be explained merely as God's

179

reckoning for sin. But in his desperation to protect the divine image from any hint of menacingness, Barth wrongly projected the sources of human distress away from God altogether and into the order that God nonetheless permits to exist. Barth's commitment to the preservation of God's innocence fails to do justice to our experience of shadowedness as we face the terrors of real evil in a divinely ordered world.

4. Of all twentieth-century theologians who have sought to express humanity's resemblance to God, perhaps none has been more influential in this country than Reinhold Niebuhr. In volume 1 of *The Nature and Destiny of Man,* Niebuhr wrote of the resemblance in terms of a freedom of spirit that makes possible both a transcending of natural processes and self-transcendence. Niebuhr's concern was to broaden the tradition's manifold tendencies to articulate our resemblance to God in terms of rationality alone. Emil Brunner maintained the tradition's emphasis on rationality, but sharply concretized it in terms of a capacity for being "addressed by God" (*Man in Revolt*). Brunner's approach opened out upon a widespread modern tendency to speak of human beings not so much in terms of what Niebuhr and Paul Tillich called "essential nature," but rather in terms of God's summons to share in a common destiny, with resemblance to God the predisposition, commensurate with our freedom, to realize that destiny. For instance, Gustaf Aulen wrote that having an image of God is having as our destiny life under God's dominion, which for Aulen meant allowing God's loving will to rule the human ego (1960, pp. 236-37). And Jürgen Moltmann spoke of the image of God as humanity's future, which is a destiny to live "before the face of God" in all relations—economic, social, political, and personal. In this characterization, humanity's resemblance to God is the capacity to act on God's behalf and in ways responsible to God (1984, p. 23).

5. In Dietrich Bonhoeffer's exposition of this text, the male-female dynamic defines human relationships in their essence, and by so doing, becomes the principal analogy by which to understand the image of God itself (1933). Karl Barth pushed the text even further. In the relationship between male and female, he argued, both God's relation to humanity and the trinitarian relations within the Godhead are made concrete to human understanding (CD, III, 1, pp. 194-95). While it may be difficult to allow Barth's christology to overthrow the Priestly tradition's stress on God's unknowable holiness, Bonhoeffer's insight into the symbolism of male and female deepens our understanding of at least some aspects of human nature, even if, as we shall see, the Priestly tradition will not permit the generalizations Bonhoeffer attributes to it.

6. This point is well expressed in the language of several contemporary liturgies for the celebration of marriage. The dismissal includes such words as these from pastor to congregation: "Bear witness to the love of God in this world, so that those to whom love is a stranger will find in you generous friends." "Christian Marriage I" from *The United Methodist Book of Worship.* Nashville: The United Methodist Publishing House, 1992, p. 127.

7. That man, passing through all things, and acquiring the knowledge of moral discipline, then attaining to the resurrection of the dead, and learning by experience what is the source of his deliverance, may always live in a state of

gratitude to the Lord, having obtained from him the gift of incorruptibility, that he might love him the more (A.H., iii, xx, 2).

8. Augustine's understanding of God the Creator and of the world as created absorbed into itself the line of thought first advanced by Irenaeus, and has wholly dominated subsequent formulations of the doctrine of God in the Christian tradition. For Augustinianism, through its medieval variants, to the Reformation, into Schleiermacher and the nineteenth century, and out of the neo-orthodoxies of our own century, the sovereignty of God and the supremacy of grace triumph majestically over all efforts to speak of a created nature with any kind of being in its own right, in ways analogous to the process by which Western philosophical thinking about finite substances proceeds, at times bewilderingly but also inexorably, from Aristotle to the metaphysical monism of Spinoza. From the perspective of comparative philosophy and religion, the Christian doctrine of creation is remarkably akin to Buddhist thinking about the insubstantiality and unreality of the material world. In both traditions, the world, with all its manifold evils, and we ourselves, have no more substantiality and permanence than do our dreams. Indeed, it sometimes seems as if all that we experience and believe to be "real" *is* only a dream, perhaps a dream in God. When the dreamer awakens, there will no longer be evil, but there will no longer be anything other than God either.

PART II

1. There is an associated translation issue, for the same Hebrew word carries the meaning of both "face" and "countenance," the latter in English communicating a certain kind of expression *on* someone's face, for example, radiance, gloominess, fright, and so on. More pertinent, though, is the way the image of, and word for, *face,* is called upon to convey a sense of the *presence* of God. "Seeing God face-to-face," can also be taken to mean "experiencing God's presence" vividly.

2. The point under consideration is sufficiently important to warrant further elaboration. Once again, Hamilton proves especially adept at formulating statements about object relations theory that get to the heart of the matter. She writes: "It is crucial to the child's emerging identity that the mother is not too set in the way she sees her child and that she is also able to modify her preconceptions into apperceptions and perceptions. The mirroring experience is a transitional experience. The more an adult is addicted to the mirroring relation, the less secure is his sense of both individuation and relationship. The mirror will never give him back what he wants. It will never show more than he can see. The delineation for which the looker so desperately searches can only emerge from the foundation of a secure *relationship* between two or more people" (1982, p. 131).

There is a good deal of sound theory and advice contained in this paragraph. For a *relationship* to develop between parent and infant, the parent may set the tone for communication, but must also be able to respond to the infant's own self-presenting communication. It is especially important that the parent not overwhelm the infant (or the child at any age) either with expectations, disappointments, and anxieties, or with a quality of delightedness that freezes the infant's attention simply upon being admired, creating a Narcissus-like preoccupation that stops time, growth, and relationships altogether. And Hamilton's reference in passing to mirroring as a "transitional" experience, as we shall see shortly, contains new psychological insights into how we experience God. For all of this wisdom, however, Hamilton nevertheless seems to believe that it is the other's face alone, with its communication of "coherent, predictable and consistent" regard (p. 200), that is the crucible for self-development. Certainly, the mirror of a parent's face conveys an essential *condition* for an infant's growing into the kind of human being she or he can become. But, to borrow another consideration from theology, it does not and cannot "impute" either that nature or those capacities the infant finally will actualize. Only in *partnership*, to be sure, with one who loves him or her already, will the infant so develop a partnership in which parents constantly adjust their gaze to the infant's emerging reality and infants notice and respond to the parental gaze.

3. Children's ideas of God can and do undergo many successive transformations for the sake of doing their proper work: e.g., to provide solace, a generally missing dimension of psychiatric treatment and theory (Horton, 1981); to enhance a sense of self, of the meaning of existence, and of an ultimate destiny (Meissner, 1984, p. 180); and to ground a sense of who we are in our "internalized, affective relationships," that helps correct the negative transferences contaminating most of our actual relationships (Jones, 1991, pp. 65, 84). In all of these functions, the meaning that our ideas of God infuse into experience derives from their symbolizing, their making-present, yearned for sources of comfort in times of separation, loss, and growth. As we grow in our capacity to form ideas of God that will serve us in the ways transitional objects serve us, the content of those ideas can, and indeed, are intended to undergo significant re-working.

4. Object relations theory in psychology and "existential" forms of contemporary theology converge in repudiating modes of thinking that are held captive by a narrow, "subject-object" framework. Classical psychoanalysis betrays its bondage to such a framework when it takes its own differentiations between actuality and illusion as absolute and then consigns God to the realm of the latter. Religious believers holding out for a God who is all actuality and no illusion are no better off for their orthodoxy. Their God is an object of belief, "out there," and we are left with no helpful way of accounting for beliefs about "him" that appear *not* to correspond with "his" objective reality. By contrast, if beliefs about God are viewed as another kind of transitional object, it becomes readily understandable how and why some such beliefs go awry. As all contractors know, weak materials make for weak structures. And when we attempt to construct a representation of a "good" deity out of "bad" internal objects, the result will be an object that can make life transitions more difficult rather than easier. The God whom we represent to ourselves and others "is" *both* a contrivance of our imagination *and* that supreme architect, artificer, imaginer, and Creator whose love toward us is truly an "all-excelling" love. Beliefs about God will be consistently misunderstood if we do not respect this all-important "both-and."

BIBLIOGRAPHY

Aulen, G. *The Faith of the Christian Church*, trans. E. Wahlstrom. Philadelphia: Fortress Press, 1960.

Barth, K. *Church Dogmatics*, III, 3, trans. G. W. Bromiley and T. F. Torrance. Edinburgh: T & T Clark, 1960.

Bollas, C. *Forces of Destiny*. London: Free Association Press, 1989.

———. *The Shadow of the Object*. New York: Columbia University Press, 1987.

Bonhoeffer, D. *Schöpfung und Fall*. Munich: Kaiser Verlag, 1933. English translation found in *Creation and Fall/Temptation*, trans. J. C. Fletcher. New York: Macmillan, 1959.

Bornkamm, H. *Luther's World of Thought*, trans. M. H. Bertram. Saint Louis: Concordia Publishing House, 1958.

Brunner, E. *Man in Revolt*, trans. O. Wyon. New York: Westminster Press, 1939.

Eichrodt, W. *Man in the Old Testament*. London: SCM Press, 1951.

Feuerbach, L. *The Essence of Christianity*, trans. G. Eliot. New York: Harper Torch Books, 1957.

Gay, P. *The Enlightenment*. 2 vols. New York: Alfred A. Knopf, 1966-69.

Gerrish, B. A. *The Old Protestantism and the New: Essays on the Reformation Heritage*. Chicago: University of Chicago Press, 1982.

Greenberg, J., and S. Mitchell. *Object Relations in Psychoanalytic Theory*. Cambridge: Harvard University Press, 1987.

Grolnick, S. A., and L. Barkin, eds. *Between Reality and Fantasy: The Transitional Object*. New York: Jacob Aaronson, 1978.

Hamilton, V. *Narcissus and Oedipus: The Children of Psychoanalysis*. London: Routledge and Kegan Paul, 1982.

Hanson, R. P. C. *Allegory and Event*. Richmond, Va.: John Knox Press, 1959.

Horton, P. *Solace: The Missing Dimension in Psychiatry*. Chicago: University of Chicago Press, 1981.

Irenaeus. *Adversus haereses*. Oxford: Oxford University Press, 1872.

Jones, J. W. *Contemporary Psychoanalysis and Religion: Transcendence and Transference*. New Haven: Yale University Press, 1991.

Kaufman, G. *The Psychology of Shame: Theory and Treatment of Shame-Based Syndromes.* New York: Springer, 1989.

Kelly, J. D. *Early Christian Doctrines.* New York: Harper & Bros., 1960.

Kohut, H. *The Analysis of the Self.* New York: International Universities Press, 1968.

———, A. Goldberg, and P. Stepansky, eds. *How Does Analysis Cure?* Chicago: University of Chicago Press, 1984.

Kung, H. *Freud and the Problem of God.* New Haven: Yale University Press, 1979.

Leavy, S. *In the Image of God.* New Haven: Yale University Press, 1988.

Lewis, H. B. *Shame and Guilt in Neurosis.* New York: International Universities Press, 1971.

Loewald, H. *Sublimation.* New Haven: Yale University Press, 1988.

Lossky, V. *In the Image and Likeness of God,* trans. J. Erickson and T. E. Bird. Tuckahoe, N.Y.: St. Vladimir's Seminary Press, 1974.

McDargh, J. *Psychoanalytic Object Relations Theory and Religion.* Lanham, Md.: University Press of America, 1983.

McNeill, J. T. *The History and Character of Calvinism.* New York: Oxford University Press, 1954.

Mahler, M. S. *On Human Symbiosis and the Viscissitudes of Individuation.* New York: International Universities Press, 1966.

Meissner, W. W. *Psychoanalysis and Religious Experience.* New Haven: Yale University Press, 1984.

Moltmann, J. *On Human Dignity: Political Theology and Ethics,* trans. M. D. Meeks. Philadelphia: Fortress Press, 1984.

Morrison, A. P. *Shame: the Underside of Narcissism.* Hillsdale, N.J.: Analytic Press, 1989.

Nathanson, D. L. ed., *The Many Faces of Shame.* New York: Guilford Press, 1987.

———. *Shame and Pride: Affect, Sex, and the Birth of the Self.* New York: W. W. Norton and Company, 1992.

Niebuhr, R. *The Nature and Destiny of Man.* 2 vols. New York: Charles Scribner's Sons, 1941.

Oden, T. *Contemporary Theology and Psychotherapy.* Philadelphia: Westminster Press, 1967.

Osborn, E. *The Beginning of Christian Philosophy.* Cambridge: Cambridge University Press, 1981.

Outler, A. *Psychotherapy and the Christian Message.* New York: Harper & Bros., 1954.

Pannenberg, W. *Anthropology in Theological Perspective,* trans. M. J. O'Connell. Philadelphia: Westminster Press, 1985.

Pelikan, J. *The Christian Tradition: A History of the Development of Doctrine.* 5 vols. Chicago: University of Chicago Press, 1971-1989.

Rizzuto, A. M. *The Birth of the Living God: A Psychoanalytic Study.* Chicago: University of Chicago Press, 1979.

Schneider, C. D. *Shame, Exposure, and Privacy.* New York: W. W. Norton and Company, 1977.

Spero, M. H. *Religious Objects as Psychological Structures: A Critical Integration of Object Relations Theory, Psychotherapy, and Judaism.* Chicago: University of Chicago Press, 1992.

Tillich, P. *Systematic Theology,* Vol. I. Chicago: University of Chicago Press, 1951.

von Rad, G. *Genesis: A Commentary.* Philadelphia: Westminster Press, 1961.

Westermann, C. *Genesis*. Neukirchen-Vluyn: Neukirchener, 1968. English translation found in *Genesis: A Practical Commentary*. Grand Rapids: Eerdmans, 1987.

Wiles, M. *The Christian Fathers*. New York: Oxford University Press, 1982.

Williams, D. D. *The Minister and the Cure of Souls*. New York: Harper & Bros., 1961.

Winnicott, D. W. *The Maturation Process and the Facilitating Environment*. New York: International Universities Press, 1965.

Wurmser, L. *The Mask of Shame*. Baltimore: Johns Hopkins University Press, 1981.